Daily Training

E. F. Benson and Eustace Miles

Writat

This edition published in 2021

ISBN : 9789390439744

Design and Setting By
Writat
(An Imprint of Vij Publishiing Group)
www.vijbooks.in
contact@vijpublishing.com

Contents

PREFACE.

THE following pages contain certain rules and suggestions concerning health, and certain simple and sensible ways in which it may, we hope, be acquired and maintained at a very small expense of time and self-denial, by a large number of people who are naturally accustomed to feel not very well. The book is founded on notes made by its two authors who, though they lead for the most part very different lives, are agreed on certain broad principles of health herein set forth. One of them, for instance, eats largely of flesh-foods every day, the other has scarcely touched meat for years. But both are accustomed to feel extremely well and to undertake considerable exertion either of mind or body without experiencing any fatigue. One of them takes regular exercise, that is to say he plays an out-door game on most days of his life, while the other who abstains from flesh-foods has little practice of the sort. He will take no out-of-door exercise for several days, work very hard, and find himself perfectly fit for some severe physical test at the end. But they are both {vi} agreed that if the one abandoned flesh-foods (which he does not propose to do) he would cease to require regular exercise, and that if the other took flesh-foods (which he does not propose to do) he would not only be very ill, but would also require regular exercise. One again is seldom seen without some appliance of tobacco in his mouth, because he finds it agreeable and after an experiment of abstinence from it found that it did not make any difference, as far as he could make out, in his general health. The other never smokes at all. One again takes a cold bath in the morning, the other a hot one followed by cold sponging.

But both are absolutely in accord on far more main points than those on which their practice, at any rate, differs, and they have found it perfectly easy to write this book together without wrangling, on which account they wish to express a pious hope that the very fact that they differ in so many things may have saved them from dogmatism. For it has helped them to realize that even when they are agreed on any point it would be a sheer stupidity to hint that they were therefore right, and in consequence they only put forward the points on which they are agreed as suggestions, hoping that others after trial may also agree with them. For universal laws on an empirical matter like health are rare, and the constitutions of men are various. One ma{vii}n's meat, in fact, is literally another man's poison. But in the main the two authors are agreed. They believe that the majority of mankind habitually eat too much and habitually take too much stimulating food and drink. They believe also that most people who do so do not take enough exercise, and that either an increase of exercise or a decrease of stimulant is needed. They believe that the best sorts of exercise are not those of slow pushing movements such as are made in the use of dumb-bells, but full brisk extended movements, with much use of the breathing apparatus and the large muscle areas of the body. Similarly they are in accord as regards present systems of training which tend to treat an entire crew or team as if they were identical specimens, not as widely different specimens; in every day life also they hold that because a certain mode of diet and work suits A, it will not necessarily suit B and C, though B and C might do worse than try it. They also regard the ordinary acceptation of the word "Training" as far too narrow, and hold that to acquire a high fitness of the body is a duty which should be within the reach of everybody, since a mind housed in a fit body is far more capable of good and sustained work than when its shell is imperfect. For this end they advocate the starting of city athletic clubs like those in certain American towns, being fully convinced that these clubs, with a {viii} reasonable attention to matters of diet, would secure for the ordinary city-worker a far higher measure of health than he is at present accustomed to enjoy.

Finally, they believe that air, light and work (and here they do not mind appearing dogmatic) are three prime remedies in the pharmacy of God. And they feel sure that sensuality is bad for everybody.

September, 1902.

CHAPTER I.

INTRODUCTORY.

AMONG the many notable discoveries made by the Anglo-Saxon race during the nineteenth century there is none more curious, none perhaps which will turn out to have been more concerned with the well-being of the race itself, than that which we may broadly call the discovery of Athletics. In itself this discovery was natural enough, since the love of sport, the pitting of the wit of man against animals, or against his fellows, has always been strongly inherent among us; but after thirty years of the new *régime* we are apt to under-estimate the extraordinary difference between the average middle-class Englishman of to-day, in the matter of athletics, and the Englishman of the late sixties. For to put it generally, games have been, if not invented, at any rate nationalized since then; a large class of professional or semi-professional players has come into existence, and an innumerable company of amateurs who play games for their own sake, and for the sake of the increased measure of health which most men find that they thereby enjoy. That this movement at present is in the exuberance of its riotous juvenility, which coming years will tame and quiet, is probable, but it is also probable that with this modification will come a more scientific method of playing games, which will convert the mere animal pleasure of using muscles and lungs into a system which, by their fit and reasonable use, ensures for their users not only a greatly increased power in mere strength and agility, but a greatly increased power of mental quickness and moral strength. The discipline, the quick obedience, the endurance which were found to be necessary for the games in themselves, will be consciously used in other ways and with objects vastly more important than mere athletic excellence. In fact, the standing luck of the Anglo-Saxons is here again typified: that which they began simply for purposes of amusement, Nature is converting and will further convert into an element, not only of physical, but of mental and moral pre-eminence.

Indeed, it was time that some new strain of growth, as it were, was imported. For decades upon decades the country life of England had been gradually drained out of the country altogether by colonization and emigration, and by centralization into its towns; and the inevitable health which waits upon those who live mainly in the open air, whose diet is simple and wholesome foods, was being undermined by close quarters, insufficient oxygen, and more than sufficient stimulants, while those of the upper classes who still lived much in the country hunted six days out of the seven, and drank seven nights out of the same number. For the good old Englishman type, "one of the rare old sort," as it is the fashion to call it, cannot in the light of to-day be fairly thought to be a very efficient or wholesome specimen. In fact, instead of admiring the life which certain not very critical observers have told us "made them what they were," we ought rather to admire the wonderful constitutions nature had given them, which did not sooner break up under the extraordinarily unhealthy *régime* of riding off every day some of the excessive port wine consumed the evening before. No doubt those works of fiction which admiringly record their feats make such a class to appear to us larger and more wide-spread than it really was; it is merely the admiration which we deprecate.

But by this wise provision of nature, simultaneously with the crowding into towns (a feature, by the way, not of decadent but of increasing national energy, and inevitable to successful competition), came this new feature, the rise of athleticism, and the desire and necessity for the health which athleticism both demands and, on the other hand, brings with it. It is requisite, in order to excel at any game which demands fleetness of foot, quickness of movement, accuracy of eye, to live, broadly speaking, in a sober and rational manner. Drunken meteors have reeled and will reel again over the athletic heavens, men who are built in such iron mould that excess appears not to interfere with their excellence, but on the one hand their brilliance is but short-lived, and on the other they are in themselves exceptional; for we may say that the average scratch player at golf, for instance, will certainly not remain on that desirable mark for six months if he drinks a bottle of port every night, and empties his box of cigarettes in two days. Thus athleticism, on the whole, encourages among its million votaries a more sensible and moderate way of life than they would, but for it, have enjoyed, and by it they now, and their children in the future, will inevitably be the fitter citizens. The green fields of England are depopulated it is true, and a thicker and ever-spreading pall of smoke rises above the clanking manufacturing towns and fog-ridden skies under which the cities hum like swarming hives; but how on Saturday afternoons are the fields populated again, and how the sand-pits crumble under the illiterate strokes of delving stockbrokers, to whom at the moment the little half-hidden ball is of more importance than the miles and millions of the Rand or the salvation of their souls!

Nor is this movement confined to those who have the money and the occasional leisure to play games. When before in the history of the nation has there been such a phenomenon as the weekly crowds at Cup ties, or the rapt lines of spectators at county cricket matches, watching with the intensest interest the games they never play, and knowing the athletic history of heroes they have never spoken to? That the pleasure and excitement of betting enter into their enthusiasm is, of course, undeniable, but we do not for a moment believe that this accounts for all of it. There is something else as well, and that something is the admiration and envy of the fitness of physical excellence. Or when before was seen so curious a sight as the ordinary bookstall groaning under magazines, the sole aim and purpose of which is to teach their readers how to obtain physical strength? The "genial broad-shouldered Englishman" of an earlier day was content to be broad-shouldered; nowadays every one wants to know how the broad shoulders are to be acquired. But the "genial broad-shouldered Englishman" of an earlier day was subsequently content to recline himself on a curtained feather-bed in a most microbeous room, with windows shut; now we tear down our curtains, fling open our windows, and plunge ourselves (without knowing why, it is true) into freezing baths before we begin the work of the day.

To say that athletics are entirely responsible for the healthier way of life pursued by the average Englishman of to-day as compared to the average Englishman of forty years ago, would be of course an assertion utterly beyond the mark. On the other hand, it is quite certainly within the mark to say that athletics have appreciably contributed to it, inasmuch as they both demand, as mentioned before, a sobriety and moderation in life as an essential to continued success, and themselves directly contribute to health as well as demanding the conditions that are likely to lead to it. At the same time the science of athletics is at present in its infancy, both whether we consider them as an end in themselves (a very small affair), or as a means to an end (an immensely large affair). Even the literature of the subject, that with which the bookstalls teem, seems to be full of fallacies, to be dealt with hereafter, and to a large extent to be based on one immense fallacy—namely, that the possession of enormous muscles, and the ability thereby to lift immense weights, is in itself an object worth the attention of a reasonable man. And when one adds to this that the actual acquirement of such power is in itself not always a very safe process, possibly leading to strain and involving misuse of the muscles themselves, it is not too much to say that if this, namely, the acquiring of huge muscles and the mere power they give, at the sacrifice in many cases of quickness, and in some at the risk of positive injury, were all, such practice would be Athleticism gone crazy. On the other hand, these periodicals would probably retort by saying, "What is the use of being able merely to hit a golf ball two hundred yards, make a totally untakeable stroke at racquets, hit over the pavilion at Lord's, or put in a hot shot at Association?" To this we readily answer, "There is no use in it at all *in itself*." But what is useful is to be possessed of the quickness, not only of muscle and eye, which is necessary to such a performance, but the quickness of seeing an opportunity, and the having the body in such perfect poise, in such perfect obedience to the will, that as soon as the opportunity occurs it instantly and correctly takes advantage of it. The acquisition of mere muscular force cannot produce this, and the professional strong man who could lift a wiry golf player from the ground with one hand will, unless he is something more than a professional strong man, be easily outdriven by the other. This borders on the vital question—namely, What is the use of athletics? And the answer is that *they are a help towards training*, by which is meant not the cultivation of a particular set of muscles in order to attain excellence at a particular game, still less the cultivation of slow moving muscles of ponderous size adapted only for the moving of heavy bodies, but the fitness of the entire body to execute the orders of the will rapidly and correctly, the health necessary and incidental to this, the endurance and strength which will result from it.

Nor is this fitness, which we desire to see the birthright of the entire race, at all confined to the body only, for to have the body in subjection in this manner necessarily contributes to the mental and moral health of a man. That his mind and morals may be extremely healthy, though he does not know a cricket-bat from a golf-club, goes without saying; but that athletics, from their engrossing nature to (we believe) the average person, from the healthy fatigue which they produce, from their insistence that a man should abstain from excess of food and drink and other habits more injurious, contribute to the health of mind and morals, is, we believe, beyond question. Training, in other words, in the bigger sense in which we wish to apply the term, has for its object not only fitness for any or for every athletic exercise, but fitness for all work mental as well as bodily. Yet it is nearly as much a mistake to devote all one's time to keeping perfectly well, as it is to disregard health altogether. We believe, in fact, that certain rules of life, certain habits and certain daily exercises produce the state of body which we denote by the phrase *being in Training*, and that this adapts its owner, in so far as he is adaptable, for any work he has to do. Not that there is any one fixed mode of life, any one diet, or any one exercise which will suit everybody, but there are certain general lines of health, broad paths which should be approximately followed, or at any rate given a trial. For in these matters the personal equation must be taken into consideration, and the diet and exercise that are beneficial to the heavily-built man of fourteen stone are not only not necessarily beneficial to a light-weight, but may be positively injurious, though, of course, it is perfectly true that frankly unwholesome diet or continuance of unhealthy habits would be injurious both for the one and the other. On this point ordinary systems of training, even when in such competent hands as those who have charge of the University crews, seem to us capable of being bettered. The entire crew, broadly speaking, are treated as if they were eight identical specimens of one machine, as if what is the best for one must necessarily be the best for all. This assumption is not only not proved; it is on the face of it highly improbable.

But it is infinitely more important that a city full of folk living, by the exigencies of their work, under far from favourable conditions, should be in decent health, than that a boatful of strong young men, living in the best conditions, should be at the tip-top of excellence of which they are capable on a given morning; and in the consideration of the question of training, what we say is submitted to the attention not only of those who have some definite athletic trial in front of them, though it is hoped that even these may find something of profit herein, but of those who have to lead a sedentary life, which does not naturally suit them, and find that their health, and through their health their work, suffers. No doubt in such cases there must be compromise to a certain degree; for some persons unfavourable hours of work, or ill-ventilated rooms are practically (at present anyhow) unavoidable, but even here there will be found to be possible not only certain rules which will mitigate the ill-results that would naturally follow, but certain corrective measures which will, to some extent, prevent the ill-results following at all.

It is in the crowded life of cities that these difficulties most beset the problem of how to bring health within the reach, not of course of those who suffer from definite disease, for that is the work of doctors and physicians, but of those who in surroundings which suited them would naturally be healthy. Hard brain-work, for instance, especially in a dead and vitiated atmosphere, though it produces merely headache in some, produces in many others (both the present writers are cases in point) violent appetite, and the natural impulse is to take large quantities of solid food. The result of this would of course be extreme somnolence, and a subsequent awakening from a sleep that is as different from nature-demanded sleep as is light from darkness, with an extreme attack of general inability. Now such a meal as this, which produced in the brain-worker somnolence and inability, would very likely have produced in the man who was shooting all day nothing but an added zest for his sport. In the one case the food goes, so to speak, to the right place; in the other to the wrong one. Yet how comparatively few of us study our health even in so superficial a manner as to know that appetite, when one lives in abnormal conditions, is not by any means the same thing as appetite when one lives wholesomely in the open air. And how many fewer have the sense, even if they know it, to put the lesson into practice, and deliberately alter their diet to suit the conditions under which they are bound to live.

Again, there are many who, when able to take exercise, are healthy and fit for any work that they may have to do, in whom the difficulty, almost the impossibility, of getting it in the ordinary way in towns, produces a marked decline in health and consequently in output of work. Here, in a chapter devoted to the consideration of the question as applied to those who must live in towns, we shall discuss the possibility of athletic clubs to be brought within the means of those to whom such clubs as at present exist are not, by reason of expense and other causes, in any way accessible. For all these, also, we shall suggest such daily exercises as can be taken in a minimum of time in the minimum of space, which have for their object not the acquisition of huge muscles, but the acquisition of healthy nerves and muscles, prompt to obey, and swift to act. For these, too, as indeed for everyone, certain perfectly simple hints will be given about the use of air, and how to breathe properly, the use of water, warm to cleanse, hot or cold to brace, and hot vapour baths to counteract that persistent clogging of the passages of the skin which more particularly besets those whose life is passed in towns, where there is less air, less exercise, more dirt, and a tendency in all to indulge excessively (considering the conditions) in food and stimulants.

Within the last few decades, it is perfectly true, the strides that have been made towards the ultimate sanitary perfection of living are enormous. Vast sums of money are quite properly spent annually on securing for town and country dwellers alike, in answer to the demands made by scientific investigators into the theory of microbes, pure water supplies, ventilation and light in dwelling-rooms, systems of drainage and disinfectants, and inspections of food which shall reduce, as far as possible, such dangers as are universally incident to life and health. Yet in a way, admirable as such expenditure and research is, admirable also as are the results which have followed it, these natural provisions for health deal more with the surroundings of the body than with the body itself. Tenement houses are built on the most approved sanitary principles, but that done it is left to the discretion of the inhabitants of them (provided they do not keep pigs or poultry in their bedrooms) to decide as to how they shall live in them. Board schools are built with rooms containing so many cubic feet of air per person, but that done the teachers are allowed to keep the windows hermetically closed. Inspectors of food, again quite properly, destroy barrows of decaying fish, and impose fines on their vendors, but no instruction is given to either rich or poor as to the nature of foods, and in consequence, with the best will in the world, they take quantities of an expensive and stimulating food, when what they really need is a cheap and nutritious one. Interesting and costly experiments are made as to the bacilli of various diseases, and numberless means of dealing with them are suggested in text-books, but what is not done is to inform people, except in the vaguest manner, as to how they may prevent such bacilli finding a suitable, nay a possible, home in their bodies.

Instead, it is here our intention to go to the object itself, to the putting of the body in such condition as will render it not only, from its inherent health, far less liable to be attacked by disease, but as will make it as far as possible a fit servant of the will, ready and prompt to act, unclogged by the débris of excess, far more capable of work than was its wont, and capable, too, of better work. It will thus be saved not from disease only, but from a continual condition of being slightly unfit, even in the case of those who (rightly in comparison with the general average of health) consider themselves healthy. Nor is such a benefit, if obtainable, limited to the present, for historically it is perfectly certain that both the bodily and mental health of any one generation depend very largely on the condition of the previous generation; since habits which are the progenitors of tendencies can be formed by any one in whom the will-power is ever so little alive. Further, in this wonderful intermingling of mind and body which we know as man, there is no change possible to one which does not affect the other, and just as deficiencies of mind produce physical ill-health, so a more healthy and cleanly condition of body produces a more healthy and cleanly mind. For who shall say of how much immorality bodily stimulants and overfeeding are not the lawful and genuine parents, or for how much depression, morose spirits, and stagnated languor of mind that organ known as the liver is not entirely responsible?

Hitherto training has been, and still is, largely regarded as a sort of monopoly of the few, and is considered by many to be mysteriously connected with beefsteaks and a total abstinence from tobacco. That such practices come under the head of certain special species of training, and no doubt in many cases are admirably fitted for the production of the highest possible excellence in one or other branch of athletics, is quite possible; but what we mean by Training, by the sort of Training, that is, which is within the reach, and lies almost in the sphere of duty, of everyone, is a less specialized and infinitely more important condition, for it means, as we have said before, a condition of body that will enable one to get the most possible out of oneself, whether the work in hand is mental, spiritual, or merely physical. But in the ensuing pages it is to be hoped that the reader will find an absence of dogmatism; such at any rate has been one of the chief objects of the authors. Theories and suggestions will be put forward, for instance, about the use of simpler foods; but it is to be remembered that they are, though supported by solid evidence, only meant to be theories and suggestions worth trying, we venture to hope, in those cases where the ordinary heavy meat meal produces on its consumer somnolence and disinclination to activity. Again, in the way of exercises, certain brisk full movements instead of dumb-bells, the use of which many find laborious, monotonous and wearying, are put forward as worth a trial, seeing that in many instances they have given satisfactory results. The book, in fact, is meant to be anything rather than a beaten hedged-in path beyond the bounds of which none may stray, for this is exactly what seems to the authors to be the defect in most existing systems of training. It is meant rather to show a not unpleasant track leading, as it were, through fields, and mainly, it is hoped, in the right direction.

Finally, even at the risk of wearisome reiteration, the word "Training" throughout is to be understood not in the sense of Training for merely some special athletic event, though it includes such, but Training for the ordinary work-a-day businesses of life, so that we may be able to do them better, quicker, with more taste for them, and with less fatigue.

CHAPTER II.

FALLACIES AND DEFECTS IN PRESENT SYSTEMS OF TRAINING.

WITHOUT for the moment taking into consideration those millions of London who stifle in crowded slums, on insufficient or unsuitable food, and many of whom have inherited from birth some taint of constitution, and concerning ourselves for the moment only with those within whose reach, broadly speaking, are all the expedients known for insuring health, we should find it curious and probably depressing to ascertain, if we could, what proportion *felt well*, given they had no definite cause of ill-health which it was out of their power to remove. Many would put down their comparatively lower level of health while living in London to the fact that they were working hard. This, if true, is a sad and sobering reflection, since it would seem to imply that Nature had not designed the average healthy individual to work hard; and though it is probably infinitely better that people should work hard, and feel slightly below par all the time, than that they should devote their whole time to keeping well, yet it would be unsatisfactory if we were forced to believe that continued hard work cannot be compatible with continued good health. Many again would say that they never feel well without exercise, and that it is impossible to get exercise in London. That they can get sufficient exercise anywhere, with a very small expense of time, we hope to show in a later chapter; but, in the meantime, have such tried deliberately and unswervingly to eat far less than they feel inclined, or to use some sort of definite selection in the matter of what they eat? Others again would (quite rightly) put down their slight but chronic indisposition to an absence of air; such perhaps do not know what an immensely increased supply of air everyone can get by always keeping bedroom windows wide open.

Now to many such the idea of using training as a means of merely keeping well is probably novel. They are accustomed to feel slightly unwell—that perhaps is too strong a term—when they are in a town and at work, and having always felt thus have acquiesced in what we may call a vicious habit. But they have always understood training to mean a *régime* of fixed exercise (founded on beefsteaks), which is as impossible for them as it would also be unsuitable for them; or, in a modified form, twenty minutes or half an hour with dumb-bells every morning and evening. Many have probably tried dumb-bells; some, no doubt, reap considerable benefit from their use, but not a few, and both the present writers are among them, after giving them a good trial, loathe the sight of them. And numbers, in such a case, have abandoned themselves, with more or less content, to continuing to feel slightly below par, and praying for the holidays.

Now the use of dumb-bells and developers is becoming something of a fetish, of a cherished idol, and, backed as it is by well-known names, is a formidable-looking god to throw stones at. But there seem to the present writers to be many grave objections to such systems as are constantly followed, whether they are used by athletes or by the much larger class of those who merely wish to get exercise from them. The *primâ facie* objection in the case of both is their extreme monotony. It is necessary apparently to raise the arms slowly in turn (bending the elbow till the dumb-bell is level with the shoulder) upwards of a hundred times or more: it is necessary to do the same again with the backs of the hands out, to extend the arms from the shoulder outwards, from the shoulder upwards, to bend the wrists to and fro (still with these infernal implements grasped in the hands), to make motions as if drawing water first on one side and then on the other, to hit out, with the weight in the hands, at an imaginary foe; in fact to push, raise, or pull this weight in practically every direction that it will go, a vast number of times. "Developers" have, as a rule, the same defects; the movements are slow, and a continued effort against permanent resistance, while the greater part of the exercise which they give is not for the greater muscles. Then follow—we are intentionally vague, and wish to show only the general lines of many systems—exercises for the muscles of the stomach and of the legs. For the breathing muscles of the chest, there are also exercises which not being concerned for the most part with these dead-weights we have found generally excellent. The masters of such systems also, as a rule, advocate practising in front of a looking-glass, stripped as far as may be, in order to observe the play of the muscles. This also is admirable advice.

Now it will be noticed at once with regard to these exercises that by far the majority of them are for the arms, and that even when, as in certain of them, the object is to develop the breathing muscles, the hands still hold the dumb-bells. In other words, something like three-quarters of the ordinary dumb-bell exercises, as advised and practised, are exercises in which the stress of the movements lies on muscles of the wrist and fore-arm, biceps, triceps, and deltoid (the shoulder muscle). What is the result if the instructions are conscientiously observed? That the muscles of the arms get developed ludicrously out of proportion to the rest of the body, for no purpose as far as we can see except that of lifting and holding weights. The far larger and more important thigh muscles and calf muscles, the great muscles of the trunk and chest, have perhaps in some of these systems no more work to do, when added together, than the muscles of the arm alone. For certain games it is of course necessary to have considerable power in the arm, yet (even for games) it is of far more importance to have the larger muscles adequately developed. But granted (with certain important reservations to be stated hereafter) that such exercises are good for certain games, we contend that they are, if not harmful, at any rate most ill-adapted for the proper development of the whole body, and for supplying exercise to those who need it, particularly in town life, for the sake of health. Certain muscles, those of the shoulder and arm, are exercised out of all proportion, whereas the larger body muscles, those in fact which are particularly needed for the correct and healthful carriage of the body, so as to provide the heart and the organs of breathing and digestion with free room to work in, are left comparatively neglected. Indeed, as far as health goes, it would be probably better for the man who has to sit at a desk for six or seven hours a day to sit upright only, and take no exercise at all, than to go religiously through his course before coming to his office, and then do his work in the cramped and huddled position which is natural to many people. But, and this is an even more serious charge, some exercises recommended in certain systems, pursued no doubt by people who for years have been in search of strength, advocate exercises which are positively risky, with regard to strain on certain parts of the body, exercises in fact which might tend to increase the strength of a strong man, but would be almost dangerous for a less strongly-developed one. Again, and this objection applies to athletes even more than to the ordinary man in search of health by means of daily exercise, are not these slow movements of dumb-bells and slow steady resistance against india-rubber productive of quite the wrong sort of strength? No doubt the incessant raising of a dumb-bell above the head, a heavy pushing stroke, will tend to enable the pusher to raise greater and greater weights above the head, but does the ordinary man, does the athlete himself desire to get strength of that kind? For the ordinary man, in the first place, does the development of fore-arm, biceps, or triceps tend in any way to increase his health, except inasmuch as the exertion thus put forth certainly enlarges some few muscles and tends to produce action of the skin by reason of heat? As far as muscular development goes he would do far better to exercise the larger muscle-areas, and for the other, a Turkish bath will give him the equivalent of a week's exercising. The fallacy that lies at the bottom of this dumb-bell and "developer" work, in fact, is that large and prominent muscles imply not only strength but health. That the use of muscles tends to both is undeniable, but for purposes of health the muscles employed are mainly the unimportant ones, while for purposes of strength, valuable chiefly to those who wish to employ muscles with a view to excellence in athletics, the strength obtained is wholly the wrong sort of strength.

It is here that the dumb-bell and developer system goes utterly and hopelessly astray. Used as an adjunct, it will assist a weak muscle to arrive at a certain girth and bulk, but considered as a cause of any successful stroke at a game, it is much more an enemy than a friend. For at all games, with a possible exception perhaps in the case of rowing, as far as strength comes into the question, it comes in as a motor-power to produce speed, whereas dumb-bell exercises have for their object, as a whole, the slow pushing of gradually increased weights. A modicum of strength is of course necessary to propel anything anywhere, but the main thing, the thing to be acquired, is speed in the muscle, in order to impart velocity to the object. And the muscles of those whose sole training is dumb-bell exercise are admirably unfitted to impart it. The weights they can lift are no doubt prodigious, but we doubt whether any man reared entirely on dumb-bells (and the more he had of that diet, the better for our point) could hit a ball over the pavilion at Lord's, make a really difficult force at tennis, drive a golf ball two hundred yards, turn a fast outside back-bracket at skating, or send in a really hot shot at Association football. In fact, the more developed he was on dumb-bell lines, the less likely he would be to be able to do any of these things; the muscle acquired is of the wrong order, it has sacrificed its speed for bulk, it is the strong engine of the luggage-train, not the strong engine of the greyhound express. And if this is not so, how does it come about that some professional strong man has never yet attained immense pre-eminence in any branch of athletics, if such strength were the desirable sort? Surely in his spare moments he might send a few balls over the gasworks at Kennington, or drive the green of the long hole at Sandwich. At golf, particularly, there is no limit to the weight of his club, he may use what weapon he pleases, and since the carry of a ball is wholly dependent on its starting velocity, he with his great strength should be able to send it beyond the dreams of any medal-winner. But as a matter of fact he cannot, not because he misjudges it, for many strong men, we believe, have an excellent eye, but because his muscles, trained to overcome resistance by slow, prolonged effort, cannot act fast. Ah, if dumb-bells could speak, what a tale they would have to tell! They would also cease to be dumb-bells; this would be an advantage.

In addition to this the dumb-bell man is continually putting a comparatively long strain on himself. To hit a half-volley at cricket, to drive a golf ball is a short concentrated effort, and one in which the whole swing and weight of the body assists. But to raise an iron bar above the head is a long strain: the bar is slowly pushed up, arteries dilate, the face is suffused, the heart and the blood-vessels, though perhaps not taxed beyond what they were meant to bear—what that is one cannot say—are, at any rate, largely taxed. Meantime the arm, the function of which is mainly speed, moves slowly and with the utmost effort. From its length, in comparison to its girth, it was quite clearly designed for quickness, and yet the poor victim has been gradually trained, by means of most tedious exercises, to become a cart-horse instead of a racer. Pure gymnastics, which only turn the arms into legs, are bad enough—dumb-bells turn the arms into a lift at a second-rate hotel. It would be as sensible, in the hopes to acquire rapidity of finger at the pianoforte, to train each finger separately to lift heavy weights. Finally, what is the result if an abnormally developed man has by reason of rheumatism or other causes to drop his exercises? It is not, we believe, yet proved, but the opinion of medical men tends to show that if one has developed a muscle to very great bulk in the past, and then drops its use, a sort of fatty degeneration sets in. Cheerful.

To recapitulate, the results we arrive at are as follows: Dumb-bell and developer exercises as a whole, according to the generality of received systems, are extremely monotonous. A motion is repeated many times, for the sake of obtaining bulk in a certain muscle—in order to produce quantity rather than quality, in fact. These motions take a considerable time owing to their number, and for the most part they are dull, owing to the slowness of the movement occasioned by the weight to be moved, which, as the patient gets stronger, is gradually increased. The slowness, the push of the movement, rather than the drive of the movement, is often recommended: the movements, we are told, *should* be made slowly.

In the second place, certain muscles, for instance, of the forearm and arm, are exercised unduly, unless the truth is that the business of man is not to keep well and be fit for his work, but like Sisyphus to roll a stone up a hill. Just as these are unduly exercised, so others are unfairly omitted or slurred over, the larger and more important muscles of the chest and trunk are starved of exercise in comparison to the arm-muscles. Also in certain systems certain muscles are wrongly used: muscles that are meant for support chiefly, as far as we can judge of the purpose of the human frame, are deluded into becoming muscles of motion, with the result that the naturally quiescent nerves and tissues underlying them are improperly excited.

Thirdly, supposing that this great development of muscle (chiefly muscle in the arm) is successfully attained, does it serve any practical use whatever as regards either health or use? As far as health goes, it passes the bounds of imagination to conceive that the main organs of the body will be benefited by excessive biceps, whereas as regards strength, for all purposes except the lifting and holding of weights, it is extremely doubtful whether an increase of such strength does not imply a corresponding decrease in speed and agility. The fastest runners are not those with prodigious muscles, the hardest hitters have not a swollen biceps. The test, in fact, of fitness and power of the body lies not in measurements, but in the ability to perform certain movements with correctness and rapidity, to be able to make complex movements, to be capable of endurance, and to perform such movements with economy of effort.

Many reservations must be made, however, in what appears to be an all-round condemnation, and if we criticise the system of the most prominent of the dumb-bell advocates, Mr. Sandow, we shall certainly find a great deal to praise in what he says. His remarks about practising before a mirror, for instance, are excellent, since to observe the play of the muscles is, or ought to be to anyone with an eye for movement, of immense interest, and takes off (this he does not say) from the unspeakable tedium of the exercise itself. So, too, when he advises cold water, open windows, moderate diet, abstention from anything which disagrees, he has nought which is not advisable. Equally true, too, is his insistence on attention of the most fixed order to the work in hand, though perhaps he does not sufficiently allow for the period in which a set exercise indulged in so often as some of his, must, almost necessarily, become mechanical and automatic. For just as it would be impossible that a practised player at any game should *consciously* attend to what he is doing (he sees, for instance, a ball which is certainly a half-volley, but does not know he thinks about half-volleys at all, yet hits correctly), so after a time a dumb-bell exercise becomes (or should become) mechanical. That perhaps is its strength: that certainly is its weakness. For this reason: all exercises are, or should be, exercises towards an end. When that end is attained, there is no longer any need for them, unless the end be merely to alter the circulation of the blood; and something fresh, for the sake of stimulus and interest, should be begun. By these dumb-bell exercises, strength sufficient for the purposes of life can be no doubt attained; but after that, unless our mission is to lift weights, they are superfluous. That the muscles of the arm, that all muscles in fact should be in a state of efficiency is highly desirable, but in a sedentary life, in the life for which exercises are most obviously useful, it is the large muscle-areas, the muscles which the stillness of sitting tends to degenerate, that should be kept up to the scratch. The inability, in fact, to sit habitually in a chair in a position in which the lungs and heart will act naturally, is a greater defect than the inability to raise 56 lbs. above the head in the left hand. Practically perfect health is compatible with an abnormally weak forearm and wrist: abnormal weakness, on the other hand, of the muscles of the chest and abdomen always implies imperfect health.

Finally, the personal equation is not sufficiently considered in any system of exercise that has come across our notice. There is Chart I. for children, Chart II. for boys between 14 and 18, Chart III. for adults. Any system of weight-moving, such as dumb-bells, will never satisfactorily fill such a need as here exists, unless the teacher will see and examine personally (provided also he has the requisite knowledge) each one of his pupils. A thick-set boy of fifteen, though he weighs the same as a tall lanky boy of the same age, requires a perfectly different set of exercises to produce in him fit and robust manhood, while the tall lanky boy may be injured by exercises that are good for the average boy of his age and weight. But that there are exercises which are practically good for everybody we fully believe. Of this we treat later. Again, for people who wish to excel at games, to begin with dumb-bells seems a mistake, for it teaches first the slow movement, whereas speed of movement should come first. That they give bulk to the muscles is undeniable, and there is a great deal to be said for bulk, if only it has the power of speed. In any case these dumb-bell and developer exercises should be alternated with quick, full movements, so as to preserve the speed of the action of the muscles.

Now most people who feel the need of, and are better for, regular exercise are accustomed, when they have leisure and opportunity, to play some sort of game; and how enormously this tendency is increasing is shown, to take one instance alone, by the huge number of golf links which have sprung up all over the kingdom, and in particular round and close to London, accessible to the city man in summer for a short round perhaps when he returns home in the evening, and certainly used by him on Saturday afternoon and probably Sunday. He does not, as a matter of fact, hurry home in order to practise his beloved dumb-bells, he is not late for dinner because he cannot leave his dumb-bells, but because he will finish his round at golf. A game, in fact, is more enjoyed by most people than mere exercise for the sake of exercise. The dumb-bells are used when a game is not to be had. But these dumb-bell exercises, as we have pointed out, do not, except in so far as they may strengthen an inordinately weak muscle, improve or help a man's game, unless we consider weight-lifting a game. Six months' continuous exercise of the slow pushing and pulling order to overcome the inertia of the dumb-bell or the contraction of india-rubber will probably not lengthen his drive, since they do not teach speed of movement. That the long driver at golf may be very strong is beyond question, but it is equally beyond question that the professional strong man will incessantly be out-driven by a player whose muscles are half the size of the other's, because the latter has cultivated swiftness of movement, the former has not. It is for this among other reasons that in the chapter on exercises we advocate, at any rate, until great speed has become easy, not the use of dumb-bells—anyhow not of dumb-bells of more than nominal weight—but a system of brisk, full movements, increasing not in regard to the resistance to be overcome, but in their own complexity. They require the same concentration of attention, but they are not fatiguing, although they give full exercise to the muscles. For it is a great error to suppose, as so many do, that fatigue is a criterion of exercise, that one has not had enough exercise, in fact, until one feels tired. Indeed, the converse, or something like the converse, is more nearly true, namely, that exercise which leaves one tired is either excessive or more probably is of the wrong sort. Fatigue is, perhaps, necessary if very severe exercise has been gone through, but it is a thing not to be sought after, and if possible to be avoided. As far as it is concerned with the muscles themselves, it shows that they have been overtaxed (an automatic signal put out by nature, saying, "Stop"), but probably in many cases feelings of fatigue arise from other causes, and a very little exercise will produce it, not because the muscles are overtaxed, but because there is something wrong with other organs of the body. Morning fatigue, the disinclination to get up after a good night's rest, not from laziness pure and simple, but from genuine languor, is an extreme instance of this. But the dumb-bell user will not get over this by putting in a vast amount of work for the biceps and triceps, though a couple of minutes spent in using certain larger muscle-areas, with the accompaniment it may be of massage, which one can easily administer himself, will probably largely alleviate it. But instead he flexes the arm a hundred and twenty times, lifting to each shoulder, perhaps, in all a dead weight of 960 lbs.

Furthermore, these dumb-bell exercises, in which the weight of the dumb-bells is gradually increased, become after a year or two very severe indeed, and one would like to know the collective opinion of doctors on such a point as this. Can it be good for a man of forty-five or fifty to manipulate weights like these, performing say for half-an-hour a day a series of exercises with them, some of which at any rate entail considerable strain? And if these exercises are not good, what is he to do? If after some years of hard work at them he does drop them, does he not become liable, or tend to become liable, to a fatty degeneration of the muscles, or at any rate to an increase of fat over the muscles? In the meantime, if the course has been "successful," if the man is enormously developed in the muscles, particularly of the arm and shoulder, it will quite assuredly be extremely difficult, if not impossible, for him to change those muscles whose birth and breeding is due to these slow pushing movements that are intended to overcome the inertia of dead weight, into muscles which have to deal swift, not heavy, blows at objects which for practical purposes (golf balls, tennis balls, even cricket balls) have hardly any inertia at all. In other words, he will find it difficult to become even passably proficient at games which require rapidity of striking—and it is hard to name the game which does not—and yet entail almost no strain on the heart and arteries, in order to supply the place of those heavy exercises which he feels himself unable, without risk, to continue. Besides this, it seems not unlikely that the perpetual straining may deaden the fineness of touch and judgment so necessary in most games. But the quick, brisk movements such as we recommend in the chapter on exercises seem to us to be singularly without the disadvantages of dumb-bell systems, as regards monotony, for their very speed is undoubtedly exhilarating; nor do they admit of any risk in the way of straining, while they exercise the muscles more than dumb-bells do, though they do not so much strengthen them. They are, therefore, quite as health-giving, since health, unless a man is positively suffering from muscular feebleness, has practically nothing to do with sheer muscular strength, while it has a great deal to do with muscular fitness. On the other hand, they have this great advantage over dumb-bell systems, namely, that they directly and rapidly tend to increase the speed with which the muscles can make their effort, and thus for that very large class of people who desire to play games, and do so whenever they can, these movements are of the greatest help even in learning the game, and also in keeping the muscles in actual and *absolute* practice for the game itself. They help, in fact, the right sort of muscle, they teach the light, rapid stroke which drives a ball. For the special exercises for each game, exercises which have been tested and found of service, we shall have to refer readers to the volumes on those games, which will subsequently appear, though even in the general list given in the chapter on exercise in this volume, no doubt they will pick out some that will be of service to them, whatever game they may wish to be in practice for.

But it is to the ordinary unathletic man, the man who does not really care about being in practice for a game, that we quite as sincerely recommend them, for it is our hope that he will find them, as we ourselves have done, pleasant and exhilarating (where we have found dumb-bells tedious and wearisome), economical in point of time, though they give, so we believe, more exercise than dumb-bells do, without strain and without fatigue. But they do not, and not for a moment do we claim it for them, increase the actual bulk of the muscles with anything approaching the rapidity possible in dumb-bell exercises, and if a man happens to want a sixteen-inch biceps without delay (or reason) it will be mere waste of time for him to use them.

There are many other points in which systems of training, in common with these dumb-bell exercises, seem to be defective, which need not be mentioned here. It is perfectly true that, as a whole, men in training—say a week after they have been training—are in excellent health. But this health we soberly believe to be realisable by men living in towns, with sedentary occupations, and, as they say, no opportunity for exercise. The man who must be in London six days out of the seven, practically abandons the attempt to keep in good health, without knowing what easy aids lie ready to his hand. He has no idea how much simple treatments, in the way of heat, baths, exposure of the body to the air, can do for him in the way of enabling that wonderful mechanism, the skin, which never sleeps, but works night and day at its business of cleansing, to have a fair chance. Such a man has a cold, and acquiesces in this state of things, saying he always has a cold in February, as if he were rather doing his duty than otherwise. It never occurs to him that to have a cold *is* to be unhealthy, that in such a case there is inflammation, and the mucous membrane is working double tides to throw it off. Such inflammation, of course, must have a cause, and is usually put down, often correctly, to sitting in a draught, or not changing when wet. But when one is really well, living, let us say, in the country, and getting wet perhaps two or three times a day, one does not catch cold. In London under such circumstances many people do. Why? Not because it is London, but because they are below par, liable to attack. And it is a gross mistake on their part to acquiesce in such a state of things. It is in most cases easily remediable, and that with little expense of time, and none at all in money for doctors' bills and abhorrent drugs.

Finally with regard to training and practice for certain games, there are two fallacies, commonly considered truisms, which are worth commenting on. The first is that mere practice is conducive to excellence, than which astounding statement there was never anything less proven. It is dreadful to think of the amount of time which real enthusiasts give to lone and solitary practice without ever dreaming that what they are doing is probably merely emphasizing and making more radical an already existing fault. Such an enthusiast (and the professors of his game encourage him in it) will take half a dozen golf balls on to a lonely upland, or half a dozen racquet balls into a lonely court, and there continue with unabated zest to do things wrong. Such practice is merely pernicious.

A second fallacy, connected with this point, is that style is unattainable. For what is style? Apparent ease to the man who knows little about it: real ease to the man who does know. And this ease is—with certain exceptions, as in a *tour de force* necessary to get out of difficulties—certainly acquirable. Awkwardness and effort are, as a rule, the effect of bad teaching or no teaching. For it must be remembered that while a ball an inch above the net at tennis, a back bracket at skating, a slog over the pavilion at Lord's, to repeat instances already used, are natural, in the sense that they are compassable without misuse of the human frame, yet they imply accurate and complex movements, which no one person would guess for himself. We say "guess" advisedly, for all games are empirical.

And thus having to a certain extent cleared the ground we will pass to construction.

CHAPTER III.

EXERCISE AND EXERCISES.

IT will not in this chapter be necessary to go at all deeply into the physiological effects and changes wrought in the body by exercise, but at the same time for those interested in the subject it will be well to sketch in the merest outline the general effect of exercise, and give the reasons why (a rule so universal as to be considered as practically without exception) those who take exercise, especially when they take it in air, where there is a sufficiency of oxygen, are in better health than those who do not.

Now every organ in the body is either in itself a muscle or a system of muscles, or is controlled by muscles. That is to say, none of the infinite processes incidental not only to any movement, but to even perfectly passive life, are independent of muscular action, automatic it may be, and unconscious or sub-conscious, but still muscular.

The action of the heart itself, for instance, which is, in ordinary circumstances, entirely automatic and absolutely essential to life, consists in the alternate contraction and expansion of muscle, which sends the blood to all parts of the body; and the heart, like all other muscles, can be made stronger with suitable exercises, can be overtaxed by undue strain, and can lapse into feebleness and degeneration if it is not rightly and fully used. For the health of all muscles, apart from their proper nourishment by food and air, lies in their proper use.

All muscles which are within our reach, so to speak, which by an effort of will on our part are made to move some portion of the body, are controlled by nerves, which transmit the message, as through a telegraph wire, from the brain to the required place. By constant use it is possible, as in the case of walking (in itself a rather complicated movement), so to accustom the nerves to send their messages that, after a time, the action of the muscles become automatic, and we are conscious of no effort of will to make them work. The instinct of self-protection is another instance of this automatic use of muscles; a man will put up his arm or duck his head to avoid a blow without consciously bidding the muscles of the arm or neck to act. Not only does continued use of a proper kind give this speed to the communication between brain and muscle, but—granted proper nourishment—it gives strength and health to the muscles used; and, broadly speaking, the man who has *all* the muscles of his body in perfect working order, is physically a thoroughly healthy man.

Now the full effects of muscular movement are far too complicated to be spoken of with any completeness. Three, however, of the simplest and most obvious may be mentioned. Exercise, as everyone knows, is productive first of quickened respiration, quickened circulation, and heat. Just as an engine burns coal in order to produce the steam which moves it, so the muscles consume material in their working, and this consumption of material again gives rise to waste products partly given off (in the form of carbonic acid gas) by the lungs, which therefore are called upon to supply a greater amount of oxygen. Hence the quickened respiration. Similarly, more blood is required to feed the working part, hence the heart is called upon to supply it with greater speed. And thirdly, since exercise produces heat, and heat perspiration, the pores of the skin are called upon to open for the purpose of exudation, and pass out with the sweat many waste products.[1] Exercise, in short, develops not only the particular muscles used, but whatever muscle is used, the heart and the lungs as well (since they have muscles of their own, which are called upon to work), and it gets rid of waste products in the body by means immediately of the skin, and, if certain most important muscles are used, by facilitating the action of the kidneys and bowels. It also, as we have seen above, quickens the co-ordination of brain, nerve and muscle, until with practice many movements become automatic instead of comparatively slow. At the same time it uses up nervous force just as it does muscular force, but only temporarily, since rest and sleep automatically (and nobody yet knows how) restore both.

This brief sketch will be enough for the moment to show why proper exercise is beneficial to the body, and it will explain in a rough and ready manner why respiration and circulation are quickened, and why exercise produces (or should produce) appetite. Actual consumption of materials has taken place, and in addition waste products, which give rise to uric acid in the system, have been removed. But though in general these effects (except when from serious weakness of the heart exercise is positively dangerous) are beneficial to everybody, it does not in the least follow that any haphazard exercise is beneficial to everybody. Certain movements, which are to be highly recommended to the robust, would if they were attempted by a man whose muscles were not so developed, be either impossible to him, or, if effected, would strain rather than strengthen him. Again, the object in general of exercise is (apart from its three results mentioned above) to brisken and strengthen harmoniously, and not to cause immense development of one or two sets of muscles, leaving the others comparatively neglected. Of course, if there is special weakness in any part it may be highly desirable to strengthen that part, but as we have said above, what we may call mere "Biceps-culture" is, though charming for the biceps, as long as the arm does not get muscle-bound, no better a contributor to general health than would be the cultivation of any other one muscle in the body, while there are many which it would be far more useful to cultivate than this. For by the use of the biceps, let us say, no other organ of the body (except in so far as quickened respiration and circulation is the result of muscular effort) is directly benefited, whereas by the use of the extensive muscles of the chest in a proper manner, freedom and strength are directly procured for the lungs, or by the use of the muscles of the abdomen in a proper manner, the action of certain internal organs is facilitated.

Now the main principles on which we base the system of exercise we recommend are these. Complete development of the muscular system is aimed at, and rapid obedience of the muscles to the will. The muscles should be exercised to their full extent—*i.e.*, they should make the full movement which their contraction allows—this fast full contraction is associated with the name of Mr. Macdonald Smith—and they should also be made efficient in arrested movements; that is to say, they should be able even in the middle of a rapid full movement to stop at once, being in complete control of the will, even as a wolf, and this is one of the seven wonders of the world, can check his spring while in mid-air. How? God knows. Mere size of muscle, we believe, is in no way a criterion either of health or of the sort of strength which we consider to be desirable, and it is infinitely better for a man to have muscles of but average size, provided they are prompt and obedient, than to be a Farnese Hercules, if the bulk of muscle which he has made for himself is but slow moving and incapable of briskness. The Farnese Hercules no doubt could lift weights of prodigious heaviness, but if the acquisition of this power has been attained at the cost of speed and promptitude, we altogether fail to see how he is benefited. Correctness and control are the first objects of muscle-culture; by proper practice comes endurance, speed, and often very great muscular power. But power—slow weight-lifting power—should be considered not as the first, still less as the only object of exercise, but as a probable result. Furthermore, though the lifting of dumb-bells is exceedingly useful in bringing an exceptionally weak muscle up to the general level of the others, dumb-bell work is, in itself, slow movement, and though even its continued use may not be altogether destructive of quickness, yet it cannot in any way be considered as conducive to it. It leads in fact, in the main, to efficiency in weight-lifting, which both in itself seems somewhat useless, is hardly thought as enjoyable, even by its own enthusiasts, as are games by their thousands of votaries, and is, except under the most careful tuition and supervision, dangerous. But in these quick full movements practised either with no weights at all, or at the most with exceedingly light ones, there is no risk of strain. Again, while to judge by the letters and testimonials sent to well-known schools of physical culture (and published by them) the increase of bulk in muscle seems to be considered in itself a desirable object, the acquisition of this bulk appears even in successful cases to be a somewhat slow and laborious process, and entails more than half an hour's dumb-bell practice of slow movements every day. As supplementary to brisk movements, it is more than possible that these mere bulk-acquiring movements have their uses, but to base an entire system on them is to miss the point, so it seems to us, of the culture of muscles, if not to ruin the muscles themselves. It is also most important to see that the exercise for each muscle shall be that for which the muscle is naturally adapted; and exercises designed to bring the muscles of the fingers or wrists into their utmost state of efficiency will be evidently utterly different from those by which we cultivate the muscles of the loins, the back, or the chest. For fingers and wrists are obviously designed (and are regularly used) for far more rapid movement than the muscles of the back, loins, or chest, and to attempt to make these larger muscle areas work with the same rapidity as the fingers attain in piano playing, is to give not only an impossible task, but a most unsuitable one. Or again, to try to accustom the fingers to sustain the weight borne every moment by the muscles of the neck would even, if it were possible, utterly unfit them for the rapid movements which are natural to them. Again, the muscles of the legs are designed to bear and to move the whole weight of the body, and it is thus obvious that exercises suitable for development of the arms may be highly unsuitable for the development of the legs, which from their greater natural bulk (designed for the continual shifting and sustaining of weight) are not able to move with the flick of the wrist. And it is here also that dumb-bells and indeed gymnastics generally seem to us to go wrong. It is to the arms in dumb-bell exercise that all this slow weight-moving is assigned, while really the essence of gymnastics seems to be to treat the arms like legs, and let them bear the whole weight of the body either passive or in motion.

Thus it appears to us a truer and more sensible way of exercise to give each muscle, as far as may be, the kind of work for which it was intended: to give to the wrists, fingers, forearms, exercises of great speed, to give to the muscles of the legs exercises of speed certainly (but of less speed, since they are weight-carriers), of balance and of flexibility (thus enabling the body to start quickly in any required direction) and of sustaining power, to give to the big areas of muscle round the spine, abdomen and loins exercises that will enable them to do more easily their pillar-like work, and allow the underlying organs of the body free play, to give to the muscles of the ribs and chest that power of expansion and contraction which will enable the lungs to breathe fully at all times, and in emergency quickly, so that when greater demands are made by the working body for supplies of oxygen, they may be readily supplied without a struggle for breath. And if these things are possible—as we entirely believe—we hold that the man who has attained them through exercise will be a greater debtor to exercise than he who can lift large weights with limbs required for other purposes.

One of the very best times for exercise, and also for most people the most convenient, is early in the morning before breakfast. The body is (or should be) fresh and untired, and by exercise it is given a good start for the day, and fortified against the congesting effects of the long sedentary work which must perhaps necessarily consume the greater part of the ensuing hours. On the other hand, some people habitually devote the freshness of the morning to brain-work, for the brain like the body should be fittest then, and one of the present writers always does his hardest brain-work immediately on waking, reserving his exercise for later. In any case, it is far better to take exercise on an empty stomach than after a meal, since in the latter case the energy of the body is largely occupied with the work of digestion, which will be imperfectly, or at any rate slowly, performed, if it is taxed simultaneously by other calls on it. Again, in order to give full and easy play to the muscles, as little clothing as possible should be worn, since they are thus unimpeded in the movements, and also because, as mentioned in the chapter on light and air, there is nothing more hardening and invigorating to the body than exposure to fresh air. The exercise itself will very soon warm the body, though perhaps at first those unaccustomed to exposure will find it wiser to take their hot bath or hot and cold bath before exercise, so as to start already warmed. But all those who are accustomed to have a cold bath, and feel no chill afterwards, may safely begin with the exercises, and reserve the delightful thrill of the water for afterwards, when they are even warmer from the exercise than they would have been on getting out of bed.

Be sure also that there is plenty of air in the room, for you will use more when you are exercising by reason of the quickened respiration. Your window, it is to be hoped, has been open all night. It is really a pity to shut it. Then stand before a looking-glass, so that you may, by the sight of the reflected movement in front of you, be sure you are doing it fully and correctly, and may the more easily fix your attention wholly and entirely on what you are doing. For it is by attention that you will acquire ease and facility till, as in learning a thing by heart, the movements eventually become if not automatic, at least extremely easy.[2]

The following exercises are for the most part exercises of full contraction and full extension. The full extension should be not only made but also *held* for a fraction of time. The parts of the body which are not being used should be kept quiet and easy for the sake of self-control, economy, and gracefulness. Each exercise is from one position (1) to another (2), and then back again. This we may accompany by saying to ourselves "1-2, 1-2." As a variant, we may alter the time, and say "1-2-1, 2-1-2," and so on, changing the pace, intervening time, etc. There must be no dulness. The photographs are of people who do not use dumb-bells.

EXERCISE I.—(For the wrist and forearm.)

Clench the right hand, holding it out straight in front of you, with the back of the hand downwards. Unclasp the fingers with a snap and simultaneously move the whole hand round on the pivot of the wrist and forearm as far as it will go. Then come back as smartly as possible to the original clenched hand position. Repeat about twenty times, making the movement as quickly as you can in both directions without sacrificing correctness or fulness. Then do the same with the left hand.

EXERCISE II.—(For upper arm.)

Extend the arm out at full stretch from the shoulder sideways, with hand and fingers completely extended and palm downwards; then bend it as smartly as possible to its full extent at the elbow, bringing the hand close to the head, with its palm, not its back, nearest to the head, and at the same time clenching the fist. Go back to former position again as smartly as possible. Repeat from twenty to thirty times. Exercise the left arm in the same way. See Photograph. Afterwards both arms may be exercised together.

EXERCISE III.—(Shoulder and chest muscles.)

Bring the hands together at full extent of arms in front of the face. From there bring them quickly back till they are in a line with the shoulders, at the same time drawing in a long breath. Return them to the first position, expelling the breath. With a very little practice it will be found that they can be brought back considerably further than the line of the shoulders. Repeat ten times.

EXERCISE IV.—(Shoulder and chest muscles.)

Stand erect with the arms by the side. Then raise them slowly outwards, still at their full extent, till they meet above the head, drawing in a long breath all the time. Pause for a moment in the second position, still

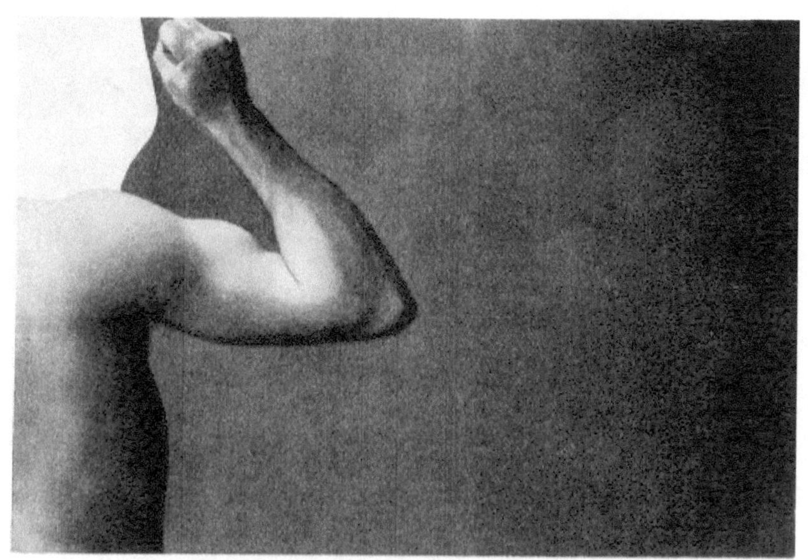

EXERCISE II.—FIRST POSITION.

[To face page 80.

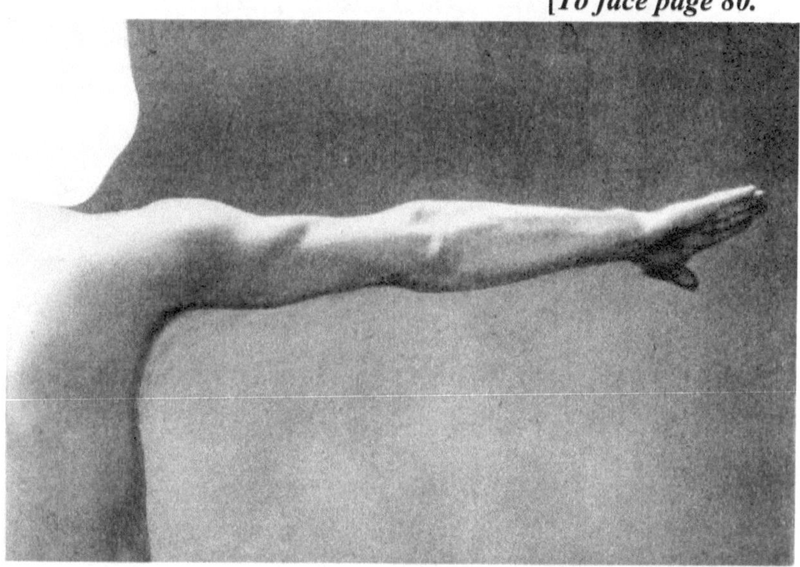

EXERCISE II.—SECOND POSITION.

[To face page 80.

41

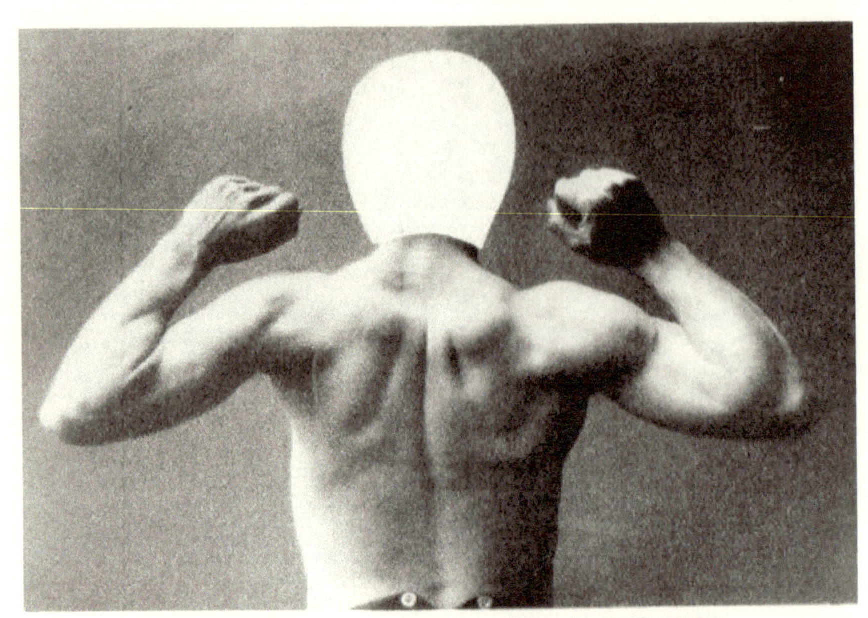

EXERCISE II.—BOTH ARMS TOGETHER.

[*To face page 80.*

EXERCISE VIII.

[To face page 81.

holding the breath, then lower the arms, slowly expelling the breath, till they are again at the side with shoulders drooped. Hold the breath out for a moment, and repeat six or eight times.

EXERCISE V.—(Breathing muscles of chest and abdomen.)

Standing erect draw a long breath, inflating first the lower, then the middle, and lastly the upper part of the chest. Hold the breath a moment, then expel the air, first emptying the lower, then the middle and then the upper part of the chest. Hold the breath out for a moment, and repeat six or eight times, stopping directly there is any feeling of giddiness.

EXERCISE VI.—(Muscles of the ankle and calf.)

Stand on each foot in turn and with the other pointed in front, bend the ankle upwards and downwards, and from side to side, and then in a circling movement, to its full extent, as rapidly as possible. Repeat about twenty times.

EXERCISE VII.—(Muscles of the knee and thigh.)

Stand on each foot in turn, and flex the knee as smartly as possible backwards to its full extent. Bring it back, heel down toe up, to its full stretch. Repeat ten times.

EXERCISE VIII.—(Balancing exercise for muscles of thigh and calf.)

Stand on one foot, and bring the other slowly upwards and forwards to full extent of the leg, bending the body back to preserve balance. Draw the leg back till it is reaching out to its full extent behind the back, leaning forwards at the same time with the body, and stretching out the arm corresponding to the extended leg to its full extent. Repeat with each foot half a dozen times. See Photograph.

EXERCISE IX.—(Muscles of ankle, knee and hip.)

Stand on left foot and turn the right inwards till the toe is at right angles to the side of the left foot. Then reverse it as smartly as possible to its full extent so that the heel of the right foot is touching the side of the left, and the toe pointing at right angles outwards. Repeat ten times with each foot. See Photograph.

EXERCISE X.—(For hips and abdomen.) (From *Health and Strength*, April, 1902.)

Stand straight, heels together, hands on the waist with thumbs to the back and fingers pointing forwards and downwards. Then keeping the legs still and the head facing forward all the time, sway the body round and round, going as far back, as far forward and down, and as far to the sides as you can. Do this slowly and see that the abdominal muscles feel a strong play, and make three circles with the trunk. Then stand still and straight again and stretch the body as high as you can, but without rising off the feet, so that the leg muscles have perfect rest. Stretch out and up after every three circles, and stop the moment the slightest feeling of tiredness comes.

[If this exercise does not seem to suit the individual, then it may be preferable to make a swift movement as

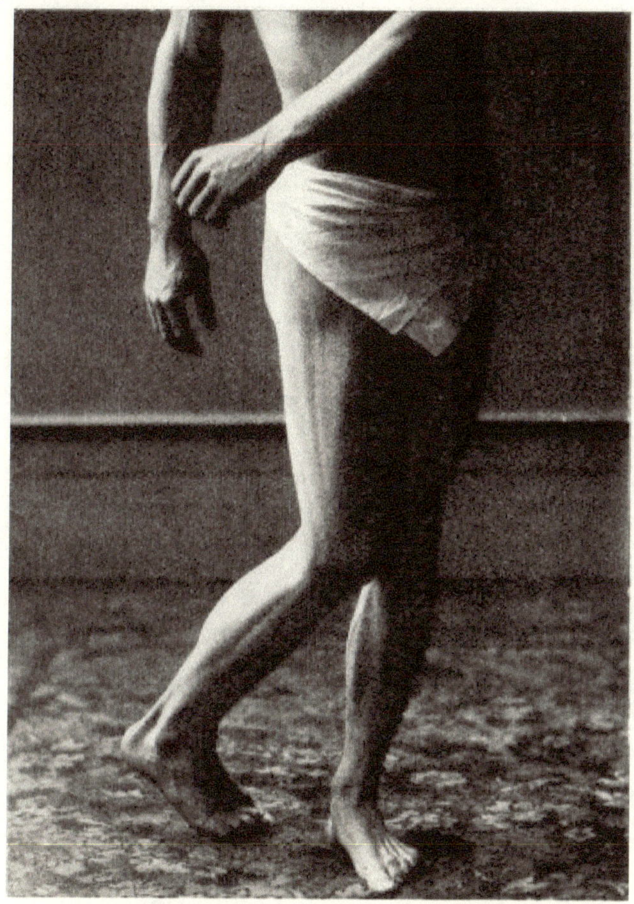

EXERCISE IX.—FIRST POSITION.

[*To face page 82.*

45

EXERCISE IX.—SECOND POSITION.

[To face page 82.

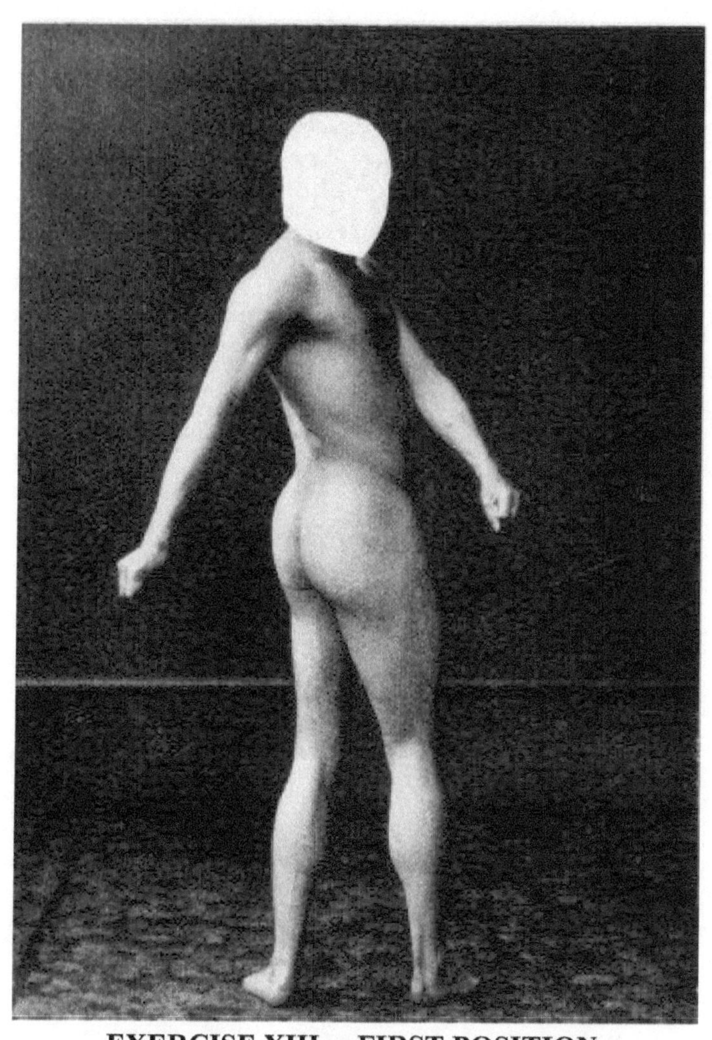

EXERCISE XIII.—FIRST POSITION.

[*To face page 83.*

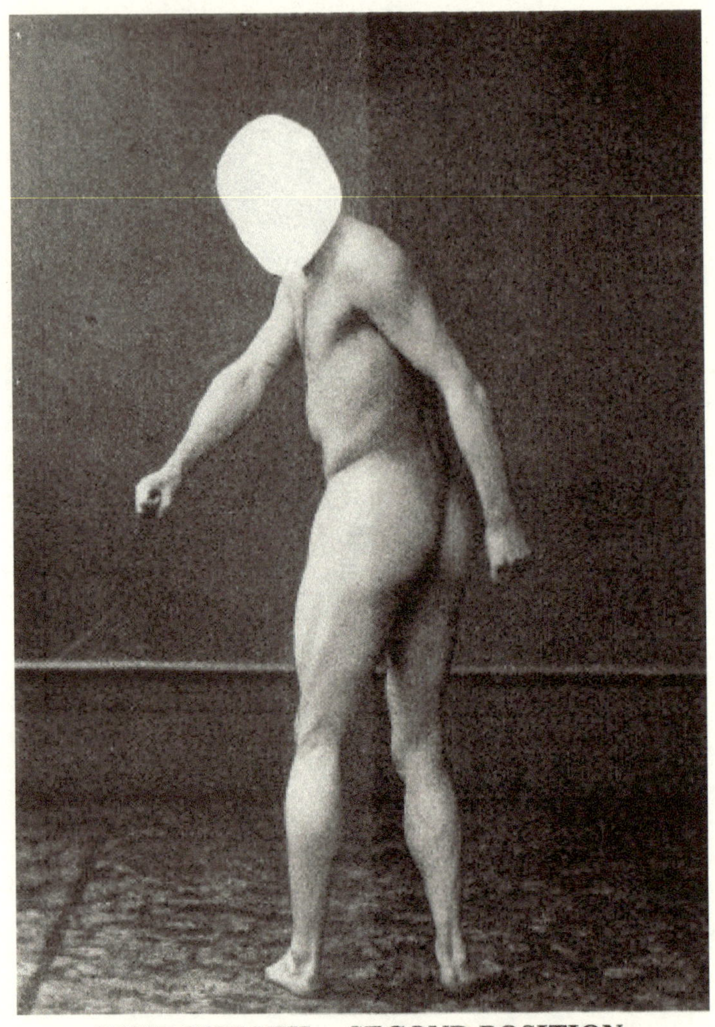

EXERCISE XIII.—SECOND POSITION.

[To face page 83.

if to pick up objects from the ground first in front of you, then on one side, then on the other, then above you.]

EXERCISE XI.—(For muscles of the trunk and back.)

Stand firm on both feet all the time, and keeping the head facing forwards, swing the trunk round first to the left and then to the right, letting the arms move freely to help the swing. Do not strain, but try to increase the extent of the turn gradually day by day. Repeat half a dozen times.

EXERCISE XII.—(For muscles of back and leg.)

Lie flat on the floor, with hands clasped behind the head. Draw right knee sharply up towards the chest, then kick it back to the full extent of the leg, stretching out toes as far as they will go. Do the same with left foot, and repeat ten times.

EXERCISE XIII.—(Neck and trunk and shoulders.)

Stand with feet and knees straight. Then turn the head round with moderate rapidity as far as it will go to the right, letting the body follow it. Remain for a moment, shrug the right shoulder, and revert the position, turning the head as far as possible to the left. Then shrug the left shoulder. Repeat six times. [With this exercise too great speed of movement should not be attempted at first, until the muscles of the neck have become pliant with exercise. Before long, however, the head can with ease be turned so far round that the eyes will cover a *circle and a half.*] See Photograph.

EXERCISE XIV.—(Combined exercise for arms, legs and trunk.)

Stand in an easy position, slightly sideways, the weight on the left foot. Then take a rapid stride forward with the right foot, the toe of the left still remaining on the ground, and simultaneously lunge forward as rapidly as possible with right arm to its full extent, following it with a forward and downward motion of the body. Recover smartly to the original position. Do the same with the left foot and arm, repeating ten or twelve times. Later on the lunge can be made in other directions as well as straight forwards.

Now this list of fourteen exercises which we have extracted from a much larger number will, we believe, be found sufficient to exercise in a healthy and reasonable manner a very large proportion of the muscles of the body. They may seem, especially to anyone who has been accustomed to long exercises with heavy dumb-bells, mere child's play, but if they are given a trial, and especially if the utmost rapidity is used in making those movements where

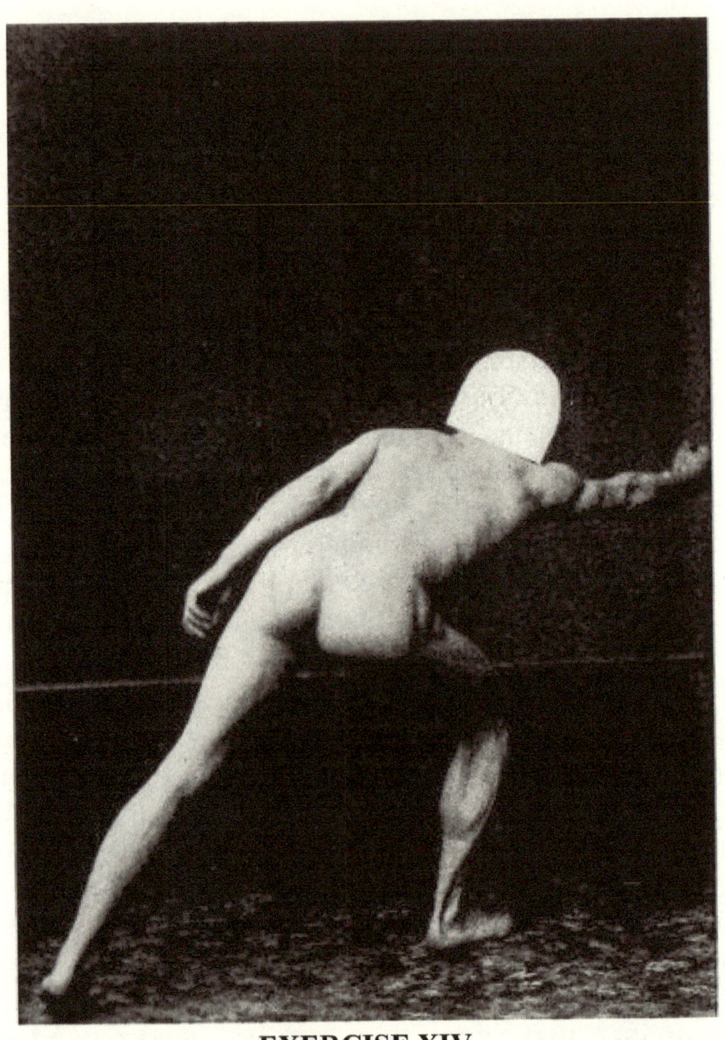

EXERCISE XIV.

[To face page 84.

rapidity is enjoined, they will, we think, be found not unsatisfactory. Those people who are accustomed to gauge their exercise by the fatigue which it produces may not, it is true, be pleased with them, but for our part we do not for a moment believe that fatigue is any criterion of satisfactory exercise. It is perfectly easy to fatigue oneself in a very few minutes by unsuitable exercises, just as it is easy for a man accustomed to walk rapidly to feel real sensations of fatigue if he has to walk very slowly for half an hour. Yet no one would say that he had therefore enjoyed more satisfactory exercise. For to use a muscle wrongly is in itself fatiguing, and for this reason exercises of the muscles of the arms should be far more rapid than exercises for the legs, and exercises for the legs in the same way more rapid than those for the chest and abdomen. It would be out of the question to try to make the breathing muscles exercise themselves with the rapidity that is easy to the muscles of the ankle, and in the same way it is useless to exercise the muscles of the wrist only as fast as it is reasonable to exercise the muscles of the abdomen. They are adapted for widely different purposes; use then each for its own.

The advantage which we claim for such exercises is that they give exercise and do not produce fatigue. Furthermore, they take far less time than ordinary courses of dumb-bell exercise, they require no apparatus whatever, they produce briskness of movement, and will keep the muscles in better condition for games and athletics than do mere slow strength-producing movements. But we should not for a moment urge a man who played games regularly to use at any rate all these exercises on those days when he is playing, for it is certain that some muscles, if not all, will be quite sufficiently exercised by the game, and thus it is mere waste of time on his part, and unnecessary expenditure of energy to add to that which is already sufficient. On the other hand, most games—at any rate as they are played by most people—will not exercise all the muscles which even this list covers, and a man might with advantage exercise those by these means.

With regard to the increase in the number of times each exercise is done, it is quite impossible to lay down any general rule, since anyone whose muscles are already accustomed to rapid movement will be able to increase the exercise more quickly than one who is not; but as a general guide for everyone it may be said that none of the exercises should be repeated more than once or twice after the least feeling of fatigue or aching begins. But far more important than mere repetition is the rapidity of movement with which one does those that are meant to be rapid, and it is infinitely better to do such exercises only half the number of times suggested, with concentration and speed, than twice the number if they are done slackly or not fully. The first essentials are to do them correctly and rapidly; the endurance and strength to repeat them many times with correctness and rapidity will come of their own accord. But the correctness is also a *sine quâ non*: for it is the intelligent and faithful obedience of the body to the will which is no less an object of exercise than the efficiency of the body considered by itself, and just as to practise these exercises correctly is the foundation of a good habit, so to practise them incorrectly is the foundation of a bad one.

For athletes, then, we believe that they will help in a marked degree to keep the muscles in good tone when there is forced on them a period of inaction from games. This effect would not be obtainable from dumb-bell exercises, since the latter for the most part are slow movements which are not of the least good as practice for games, but (though undoubtedly strength-giving) if used alone rather prejudicial to speed than otherwise. And for non-athletic people and athletes alike, they will help to keep the body in good health, not only because, for reasons given above, exercise is healthy, but because many of them are specially devoted to using those large muscle-areas of the body on which the proper daily working of the system depends, and these are exercised without risk of straining, whereas to exercise them with heavy dumb-bells in the hands has before now produced, and will again produce, injury. Furthermore, the body is far less liable to be attacked by definite disease if it is in a healthy condition, while also the daily hardening which it will experience in the system of exposure which we recommend, will render it considerably less prone to catch cold by reason of draughts or change of temperatures, which otherwise are often the immediate causes of chill.

Now, though games are more to be recommended than mere exercise for those who can afford the time and money for them, inasmuch as the enjoyment derived from them is greater (the benefit derived being therefore greater),[3] and all sorts of qualities are called out, which mere exercises do not demand, it must not be supposed that all games (or for that matter all exercises) are suitable to all ages and constitutions. For in the human body speed (as in these exercises) is naturally developed before strength, and a lad of twenty will beat a man of forty in a hundred yards' race, though he has not nearly the same amount of pure physical force at his disposal. Short and violent exercises, exercises demanding top speed, or a swift stroke, are natural to youth, and, broadly speaking, as with advancing years (even though a man is still in his prime) strength increases, speed somewhat diminishes. Thus, though exercise and exercises are quite undoubtedly good for a young boy, it seems by the example of nature herself, that exercises demanding strength and continued effort are bad. Thus for children we should never recommend dumb-bell or developer exercises at all, except with weights and resistances so small that they practically call forth no extra strength to manipulate, but which serve in so far as the hand is occupied to fix the child's attention on what he is doing. Even in later years strength, or at any rate that sort of strength which is measured and accompanied by very bulky muscles, not only does not assist, but even hinders speed of any movement; and though a certain amount of strength is required for movement of any kind, it is (though it is possible not to have enough) also possible to have too much of the wrong sort. Of course, if a man's physical ambition is limited to weight-lifting, there is nothing more to be said: let him continually lift weights. But if it is in the direction either of good health or athletic excellence, we think he can do better than practise habitually with dumb-bells, or "grips," or other strain-producing apparatus.

Finally, exercise in company with others is more entertaining and likely to be then done both better and more beneficially than exercise practised alone, and it is with this among other objects that we have advocated in the chapter on Mind and Morals the formation of city clubs where both practice-exercises like those given above could be done in classes, and also such games as squash, badminton, fives, and covered tennis be played. In the separate volumes which deal with individual games will be found special practice-exercises for those games, some of which can take the place of the general exercises given above, since they exercise the same muscles, but in a way more directly adapted for the games in question.

CHAPTER IV.

DIET AND STIMULANTS.

DOGMATISM on any subject is dangerous: in matters of food it is fatal. One man's meat is literally another man's poison, and because one of the writers knows that personally he can digest without the slightest discomfort a heavy supper, sleep the sleep of the just, and rise cheerful and hungry for breakfast, he would be making a great mistake in recommending such a course for a dyspeptic person, with a view to the strengthening of his digestive processes. In fact, if a naturally dyspeptic person persevered in such a system, this unfortunate scribe would probably be summoned to attend—with shame and dishonour—a coroner's inquest. On the other hand, should the dyspeptic so far win him over as to make him give what he would call a "fair trial" to a simple diet, "the only diet" he would say "on which it is possible to keep fairly well," he would, if it was persevered with, be probably asked in a public place what he knew about this suicide. But the moral of these gloomy reflections is clear enough: namely, that in questions of eating and drinking and smoking, what is to be ascertained is the diet which will keep A or B in good health for the proper performance of a citizen's duties. Whatever diet (or absence of diet) continues to give good results after a protracted trial is almost certainly good for the individual in question. Whether it would be good for another individual it is impossible to say, but if any one person, even though he lived exclusively on green cigars and Egyptian mummies, continued to be in his most excellent health on such a diet, it would be foolish to urge him, except on the score of expense in the way of import duties, to change it.

But the majority of people are not at their best, and know it. When they are in hard work which, as far as we can see in the present highly competitive state of the world, is becoming the normal condition for man, their bodily health, and in particular their bodily activity, sensibly declines. Then perhaps there comes a lull, and they rush off into the country to be out of doors all day, and play games, or shoot or hunt, and get sensibly better. They have more appetite for food, and as a natural consequence digest it better, since wholesome appetite is a fair enough sign-post pointing to the pleasant place called "Eat." Then the lull ceases; they go back to work again, with a gradual decline of appetite. At these cross-roads, so to speak, for the most part they take the wrong turning, and continue to eat much as before. Horrors ensue.

The fact is that most people when taking a great deal of exercise are able to digest, and, what is not less important, to assimilate, not only larger quantities of food than they can assimilate when in full sedentary work, but a different sort of food. As a rule they know of only one change of diet, alluded to contemptuously as "Vegetarianism," and connected in their minds with huge platefuls of damp cabbage, of which the most valuable salts have been boiled out and thrown away by an ignorant cook. They are further "put off" by what appears to most people preposterous notions about the sin, no less, of eating animal food. In fact, bad cooking and tactless enthusiasm have hand in hand done their utmost to ruin the vegetarian cause. To eat damp cabbage can be, by no conceivable process, good for anybody, and to shun animal food because it implies death to an animal is a motive which does not appeal to the majority, who, without examining any possible truth it may contain, label it a fad. And there is nothing which in the minds of ordinary people, who most naturally and sensibly do not wish to spend the whole of their lives in discovering the diet which best suits them, is more strongly prejudicial to any examination of a new system than to suspect it of being faddy. They naturally desire a *régime* of which the common-sense appeals to them, and the common-sense of that which is ordinarily called vegetarianism is far to seek. Many people have found that the amount of meat which they usually eat is not very good for them: that three flesh meals a day are excessive in the way of animal food; on the other hand they must have something substituted for the meat, and they turn to vegetarianism, and perhaps try a meal at some vegetarian eating-house. One of the present writers tried it. For an hour or rather less he felt that he would never eat again as long as he lived, then, almost without transition, he felt that he wished to eat the whole world round. And he fled back to the fleshpots of Egypt.

But nowadays vegetarianism is studied by certain people in a spirit of scientific investigation, and its results, rationally arrived at, are likely to prove of the most permanent value. It is the greatest possible mistake to suppose that all vegetables and fruits are equally supporting; some are highly nutritious, others are hardly nutritious at all, and to load the stomach with immense masses of a food which has a low nutritious value, in order to get sufficient nutriment, will probably produce results on health worse even than those from which the man who found that he was taking excessive quantities of animal food tried to escape.[4]

Briefly, then, the scientific view of food in general is as follows.

Food has to supply waste of tissue and make repairs.

Food has to supply heat (fuel for the continual combustion of the body) and a certain amount of fat.

Food—so it is usually asserted and largely believed—has to give the stomach a certain amount of fibrous matter to supply bulk which will enable the system, by natural means, to cleanse and flush itself internally, and throw off the waste for which it has no use, but which exists in greater or smaller quantities in all foods.

Incidentally, also, food should be of such taste and nature as easily to excite the saliva, which is almost indispensable to procure digestion.

Now the one great necessity without which we die is proteid, because proteid supplies (and nothing else in the world supplies) the waste which daily and hourly goes on in the body. It is present in conveniently large quantities in all meat foods, which is one of the main causes of their being eaten, but it is present also in large quantities in cheese, milk-proteid, grains, nuts, and pulses, though in certain other fruits and vegetables it is almost completely absent. It would be practically impossible, for instance, to eat enough cabbages to supply the necessary amount of pure proteid per diem, which must, and this is important, not only be swallowed but be digested. On the other hand, it is easily possible to get enough proteid per diem by a meat diet, but it is even easier to get enough from a diet of grains, nuts, pulses, and milk-proteid,[5] provided the right sorts are eaten.

The following abridged table giving the values of certain common articles of diet both in proteids and also in fattening and heating products will make this clear.

TABLE OF FOOD VALUES.

(ABRIDGED FROM "FAILURES OF VEGETARIANISM.")

Foods—uncooked, unless otherwise stated.	Proteid.	Fat.	Carbo-hydrates.	Salts.
Beef (with moderate amount of fat)	20.	1.5	...	1.3
Mutton (with moderate amount of fat)	14.5	19.5	...	0.8
Pork	12.	26.2	...	1.1
Fresh fish	10.5	2.5	...	1.
Milk	2.3	4.	4.5	0.7
Plasmon	69.	...	...	8.5
Cheddar cheese	33.4	26.8	...	3.9
Eggs (white)	12.6	0.25	...	...
Eggs (yolk)	16.2	31.75	...	...
Hovis bread	9.9	1.6	42.3	1.2
Wholemeal bread ("Manhu" is similar)	6.3	1.2	44.8	1.2
White bread	6.5 to 3	1.0	51.2	1.0
Boiled rice	5.0	0.1	41.9	0.3
Macaroni	10.89	0.45	76.05	0.64
Dried peas	21.0	1.8	55.4	2.6
Lentils	23.0	2.0	58.4	2.7
Haricots	23.0	2.3	55.8	3.2
Potatoes	1.2	0.1	19.1	0.9
Turnips	0.9	0.15	5.0	0.8
Onions	1.6	0.3	6.3	0.6
Cabbage	1.8	0.4	5.8	1.3
Tomatoes	1.3	0.2	5.0	0.76
Cucumbers	0.81	0.1	2.1	0.4
Apples	0.4	...	12.5	0.4
Plums	1.0	...	14.8	0.5
Cherries	0.8	...	8.9	0.5
Strawberries	1.0	...	6.3	0.7

Bananas	1.5 to 3	...	22.9	0.9
Lemons	1.0	...	8.3	0.5
Dried dates	4.4	...	65.7	1.5
Dried figs	5.5	...	62.8	2.3
Chestnuts	10.1	10.0	...	2.7
Walnuts	15.6	62.6	7.4	2.9
Sweet almonds	24.0	54.0	10.0	3.0
Cocoa bean	6.3	50.44	4.20	2.75

It is obvious then, that as far as the theoretical reasons for eating food at all are concerned, it is perfectly easy to obtain all the essentials for support without touching animal food, and without in any way loading the stomach with unnecessary bulk; and leaving out of the question, for the present, the economical advantage of adopting these simple foods, there is one enormous advantage which they possess for many. These are they who, especially in town life, and when they are not able to take the requisite amount of exercise, suffer chronically from slight biliousness or congested liver, and the depression attendant thereon, who feel sleepy or fatigued when in better health they would feel neither. Their ailments may rarely or never amount to what they would call "an attack," but habitually they are slightly clogged. Now in nine cases out of ten this feeling is due to the presence of uric acid in the body, which is produced in larger quantities than the system, without the aid of daily perspiration, which gets rid of acids to a large extent through the skin, can throw off. This uric acid is a product of waste within the body, and the foods which cause it are (to a much larger extent than all others) flesh foods.

Many people know this without knowing it; in other words, many men who have an attack of biliousness, lumbago, or gout (all direct results of the presence of uric acid in the body), at once cut off, even without consulting a doctor, their daily consumption of flesh. But then their ignorance makes them suffer, for they most likely in the curtailment of flesh-food do not take enough proteid, with the effect that after a day or two of such treatment they feel lowered. Naturally: they have been starving. And the lowered feeling they put down to the absence of flesh-food, whereas it is chiefly the absence of proteid from which they are suffering. They could easily have avoided this by eating instead of flesh some of the fleshless foods which are valuable in proteid, and they can—humanly speaking—if the abstinence from flesh-foods, as is almost invariably the case, relieves their attack, guard against such attacks in the future, by a diet, complete or modified, of the kind which has relieved them. But, and this is highly important, it is a fatal mistake not to take enough proteid, and not to remember that it is easily possible to eat heavy meals without taking enough. Four or five ounces per diem of proteid, not only swallowed but digested, is said to be the average required.

Now there are many people in excellent health who live in the ordinary manner *i.e.*, on a varied diet including meat, and as long as they are well, there seems to be no reason, except to be humane and to save the money they spend in food—and that may be a great inducement—why they should try a new diet when their present one suits them well, except that, for all they can tell, another diet might suit them better. At the same time there are certainly many people who are perfectly aware that they have periodical attacks of liver or biliousness directly traceable to diet, and many others who put themselves down as having chronically bad digestions, with which any food is continually liable to disagree. It is to these particularly that a trial of the simpler foods is recommended, whether they are adopted *in toto*, or used to modify existing diet. Similarly, also, the simpler foods are recommended as worth a trial by athletes who are in training for some special event, to whom either economy is an object (for a most varied diet of simpler foods can be had at a daily cost of less than a shilling), or whom the present heavy though wholesome meals do not suit. Furthermore, it is quite possible, as we said, that even those who consider themselves well might be still better without flesh-foods.

Another effect of this simpler food diet is that it has been found by trial to lessen greatly the desire for stimulants. Why this should be so is a question for physiologists, and cannot be discussed here. It may, however, be taken as a fact. And those who have tried the diet fairly (and one of the present writers has lived on simple foods—*i.e.*, scarcely touched meat in any form for some years) find that abstinence from meat directly increases the activity and promptitude, not only of the body, but of the mind, while both mind and body are capable of doing far harder and better work than before. The simpler food diet by itself will probably be found adequate to reduce the excessive uric acid in the body to practically nil—*i.e.*, natural means will be sufficient to cope with it; but it is useful to remember that alkalis may also be used as a preventive or cure.

Another alteration in diet, which we give with the reiterated proviso that it may not suit everybody, is the habit of having no breakfast, or if any, only a fruit breakfast. A very great number of people do not feel hungry immediately on rising, and in America this plan is largely adopted even by those who have to start the day with severe physical work. For those who do feel hungry on rising it seems most probable that breakfast is indicated, but on the other hand it is more than possible that for those who do not, breakfast is not indicated. And to eat a typical English breakfast, consisting probably of fish and meat, washed down with tea—which cannot be recommended as a fluid likely to help digestion. When one does not want it, is really to require a daily miracle from the inside if one is so unreasonable as to demand that it shall dispose of these things without more ado. Similarly, to limit one's eating to two meals a day has been found by many to be a valuable aid to health, though others, on the other hand, find that the quantity they really feel that they require, if they only eat twice, is apt to overload the stomach.

Again, it is probably not good for anybody to take violent exertion of the body, or do headwork immediately after or before any meal. With many people it is unfortunately impossible to prevent this; a man's only free time for his exercise may be immediately after lunch, or he may have to continue his deskwork till immediately before. In such cases this must be taken as a necessary evil; for exercise even immediately after a meal will probably be better for a man than none at all, while not to work up to the meal may mean neglect of work, which is more culpable than indigestion. For such, a light meal is strongly recommended, and in particular a meal as free of flesh-foods as the eater can manage.

It is of the greatest importance that whatever diet is found to suit the individual taste, this diet should be eaten slowly and thoroughly masticated, otherwise the most suitable and wholesome food may both disagree with the eater, and lose most of its nourishing value. Nuts are a good example of this—they have an odious reputation for indigestibility which is quite unfounded, for they are perfectly easy of digestion to most people if only they are very thoroughly masticated. But swallowed in large pieces, in any pieces in fact except the smallest, they are exceedingly indigestible. Similarly, also, many nuts are extremely rich in proteids (the chestnut, for instance, containing 14·6 per cent., the peanut[6] upwards of 28 per cent. of proteid), but in order to *get at* the proteid they must be bitten almost to powder and thoroughly mixed with saliva. Otherwise they are not distributed (*i.e.*, digested), but are passed through the body in the same way as chests of gold (securely fastened up) can be sent by train, so to speak, through a country without enriching it. It is of equal importance thoroughly to masticate all starchy foods (bread, potatoes, &c.), so that the saliva may penetrate them and begin the work of digestion in the mouth, and it is largely for this reason that doctors recommend toast or biscuits to dyspeptic patients rather than bread, because it is impossible to swallow crisp toast without properly biting it, whereas lumps of soft bread can be swallowed without actual pain. On this point we adopt a fearless dogmatism, and assert that it is good for nobody to swallow unmasticated food, both because the act of mastication is part of the digestive process, and because mastication itself renders the nutritive elements of the food accessible to the stomach. Thus less bulk of food is needed, there is less waste, and the digestive juices of the stomach are not, so to speak, called on to make violent assaults on what they receive, to behave like burglars, wresting what is valuable from the food. The burglary is done by the teeth, which, by the way, seem to be kept in better repair by mere mastication than by any other means, and the energy otherwise used by the stomach remains undrawn upon. Also, if one bites food well it is far easier to know correctly when one has eaten enough; lumps of food bolted are for the time being "locked up"; it is uncertain whether they are going to satisfy hunger or not. Even if unnutritious they will produce a feeling of satiety for the time being, and an hour later they may be found wanting. A certain amount of bulk, as we have said, is needed, but beyond that the richer a food is in the desired qualities of power of repair, and of supply of energy, the better is that food, provided it is easily digestible. And its full value cannot be brought into play, especially in the case of starhy foods, without thorough mastication.[7]

As to drink and stimulants more regard if possible must be paid to what we have called "the personal equation" than even in matters of food. Excess of everything—for such is the implication of the word itself—must be bad for everybody, but there is no earthly foundation for supposing that what is excess for one person injures another in the very least. A shower of rain ruins a picture-hat in a few moments: the same shower does not practically injure a locomotive engine at all, and is absolutely good for sprouting corn. Alcohol for instance, if indulged in at all by one man, will assuredly lead either to excess or to inordinate craving for it, while another man will drink wine at lunch and dinner for years without ever feeling the slightest desire to increase his usual quantity. What he drinks, again, would hopelessly disagree with, or perhaps intoxicate another man, while it seems as far as we can judge to suit him; he would perhaps even be definitely less well without it. It is on this point that preachers of total abstinence, just like vegetarians, are often their own worst foes. They seem to regard the process of fermentation (a natural one after all) as productive of something which is in itself immoral. Drunkenness, of course, is a vice; we all know that; but so, and certain teetotallers seem to forget this, is gluttony. They each of them turn man into a brute beast, though what many teetotallers would look approvingly at as "a good hearty meal" appears to us to partake fully as much of the nature of debauchery as does the drinking of a bottle of champagne at dinner. The question of drinking, in fact, seems to us one that each man must settle for himself, by finding out experimentally whether he needs stimulant or not. Probably the healthier he is the less he needs it, and to spur a horse that is already going as well as the rider has any right to expect is both a cruelty and a false use of energy. It seems certain, also, that most people who take stimulants at all take more than they really need, partly because of the pleasant effect of stimulant in the heightened vividity it gives (leaving anything like drunkenness out of the question), and because of the taste of alcoholic beverages, which nine out of ten people find most palatable. Here again preachers of total abstinence put forward an argument so silly that it is scarcely worth combating (were it not for the fact that it is so often repeated), when they say that what we have called "heightened vividity" is the thin end of intoxication. It is nothing of the kind. Food itself is a stimulant as well as a nutriment; a mutton chop or a welsh rarebit when one is hungry gives heightened vividity; so also does whisky and soda.

But, and here we tread more sensible ground, it must be remembered that alcohol is *not* a nourishing stimulant, and that its effect quickly wears off, leaving reaction, however slight, in everybody. Nor must we keep out of the question what the continued effects of alcohol are. Its bad results may not be apparent for a long time. In certain cases there are bad results; in certain other cases apparently there are none. Authorities on training are universally agreed that very little, if any, should be taken when the training has begun; and they are unquestionably right, because the object of training is to produce before a certain date or during a certain period a specimen of manhood at its highest possible physical level, strung up and maintained at concert pitch. To do this the whole structure must be sound, and stimulant then appears to be of the nature of a temporary prop, which has again and again to be set up afresh. Also, repeatedly applied stimulant followed by repeated reaction is not ideal.

The same remarks apply to the ordinary individual in a less degree; for though he should aim at ideal health, he does not want the sort of health which a boat-race crew want. In fact, in a necessarily sedentary life it would be exceedingly inconvenient to him; for to maintain it it seems necessary to have hard daily exercise, quantities of open air, and hours which are practically impossible for the ordinary man who has to do his daily work. An abstemious man who has been accustomed to alcohol may easily, if he drops its use altogether, find himself continuing to desire it, at an expense of nervous fretting which will cost him more than the possible gain in health may be worth. But when any man who takes alcohol finds himself desiring it more and more and in increased quantities, if even at one meal, let us say, he is unable to get it, and finds himself fretting for it, we have no hesitation in begging him at whatever cost to drop it altogether and at once. We do not say he is on the high road to become a drunkard, but somewhere ahead of him there easily may be that high road. We should further advise everybody to try at any rate what is the effect of drinking alcohol, let us say, once a day only. Of course, the difficulty which faces most people is what to drink instead; and, as far as pleasure goes, the difficulty is a real one. We cordially recommend total abstainers to try to find a solution. Various non-alcoholic drinks have from time to time been sedulously advertised, but most of them are abhorrent to the ordinary palate, being sickly sweet.

Here comes in the question of the general regulation of drinks, which, theoretically, we are afraid, is a most uncomfortable gospel. For the effect of drinking cold things during a meal, except in very small quantities, is without doubt digestively criminal: since the result of pouring cold aspersions into the stomach while it is busy with digestion is to lower its temperature at the time when heat is needed, and also to weaken and water down the digestive juices.[8] There is no getting over this: long drinks on hot days at lunch are not to be recommended. But even here the baffled voluptuary may find a way out which is not so disagreeable. He may by all means have his long drink half an hour before lunch, or at a rather long interval after. If he choose after, he will find, especially if he has eaten fruit at lunch, that he does not want it, and that though the satisfaction of a real throatful of cold liquid is denied him, he will have taken during lunch quite sufficient liquid to satisfy his thirst. But that is the best we can do for him, and we will not insult him by saying that plenty of hot water or hot water and lemon is delicious, and so much nicer than whisky and soda iced. For it is not nearly so nice.

Finally, with regard to that other soother and strengthener, tobacco, we have no sympathy with extremists, and we assert that the moderate use of tobacco will not and cannot reduce the ordinary constitution to a wreck in ten years, while in many cases it is absolutely beneficial, at least for the time, as a nerve-sedative. Many people, one of the present writers is one, finds that he can work more steadily and with less restlessness when smoking. But, and here is a warning, if, after a spell of hard work of three or four hours, you find the ash-tray a pile of cigarette ends, most of them probably smoked only half-consciously, take steps. Put the box of cigarettes in another room, so that you have to get up in order to procure one. Then, if you find yourself wondering whether it is worth while getting one, you may be quite certain that you do not really want it. Furthermore, tobacco is not nearly so insidious as alcohol; it is perfectly easy for every one who smokes to know whether it suits him. Many people it does not suit at all, and most of them know it. Here we should recommend all smokers to try the effect of abstinence for a couple of days, or at any rate of abstinence up till dinner-time. This would separate the sheep from the goats: many—the present writer is one again—will find that apparently no good effects ensue, and a certain restlessness is the only result. Others will find themselves distinctly better both in energy and in accuracy of eye and keenness of perception. These we should recommend to drop it altogether, and for their comfort the writer can assure them that, having tried this experiment himself, he found that the craving for it lasted only a few days, and that during those few days it was always possible to neutralise it for periods of an hour or so, by chewing an ordinary dried camomile-flower (2d. per ounce), the extreme and rather pleasant bitterness of which renders the thought of tobacco literally abhorrent as long as the taste of it remains in the mouth.

But here again strict training for a special event almost, if not quite, unanimously demands a total abstinence from tobacco from the beginning of training. The use of this we confess ourselves utterly unable to see, since we do not believe at all that, as in the case of drink, to take a little necessarily means a desire for more, but rather the extinguishing of the desire for the time being. The case is, in fact, in our judgment, a parallel to the shower of rain on the locomotive: it is inconceivable almost that it should do so much harm as its uncompromising opponents assert, and in many cases we believe its very moderate use would save a certain amount of restlessness, which in present systems of training is far more common than it ought to be. It is not in fact rare, whereas it should be not only rare, but almost unknown. For training is supposed to be the ideal way of living with a view to complete physical fitness, but under most systems severe training entails an almost total cessation of brain work, while it does not imply a total cessation of mental worry. Men often get fidgetty and stale before their weeks of training are nearly over, and this is due partly, no doubt, to the absurd system of training a whole crew, for instance, as if they were identical specimens of the same man, but also to the very fact that brain work is practically tabooed, just as tobacco is tabooed. Neither, in strict moderation, we believe, particularly brain-work, can possibly be as bad as they are frequently accused of being, and both might very possibly be found a sedative for a body that is bursting with condition. Besides, if training unfits a man for brain-work there is something probably wrong with the system of training, whereas if any brain-work unfits a man for training, it is seriously to be considered whether it is worth while to train at all.[9]

For the right training, so we believe, is that which shall enable a man—this is no fanciful idea, but one that has and is now being put into practice by both the writers—to be capable of hard brain-work during the whole time that he is putting his body into the best possible condition both for general health and also for a special event. The *mens sana* should not be left out of the *corpore sano*, and health consists in the efficiency not of one at the cost of the other, but of both to the benefit of each. Finally, with regard to special training, we believe that it cannot possibly fail to be injurious to a man to go out of severe training with the completeness and suddenness with which many do when the event is over. After a training of weeks, the desire for certain foods and stimulants, if they were in themselves unhealthy, should have ceased, the body in fact should have been brought into such a condition that it would feel by now a natural repugnance for them. If, then, this repugnance, or at any rate absence of desire is not felt, either they were not unhealthy, and might have been allowed in moderation, or the resumption of them with that extreme freedom—not to say excess—which marks the end of training, is only compassed with a certain effort. Is it worth while?

Finally, also, with regard to general training, the acquirement that is of really good health, which is within the reach of the majority, and incumbent upon all to attempt, a fair trial of simpler foods is recommended to all who habitually feel slightly indisposed when working hard, and who are cut off to a large extent from regular exercise, and is suggested, if only on the ground of expense, to many others. Similarly, a diminution in stimulants is recommended to all who habitually take them, in order that they may find for themselves what the effect (on themselves only) is. Similarly, also, with regard to smoking: for the concensus of professional trainers is dead against it, as a foe both to eye and endurance. Some, we believe, will not find it so, but anyone may, and very likely the majority will. In any case, it will hurt nobody to drop it for a week or two.

CHAPTER V.

WATER, HEAT AND LIGHT.

IT is not our intention to speak in any special manner about prescribed remedies for different ailments, since our concern is with the general standard of health and fitness rather than with temporary ailments, for which in many cases some special treatment is the most convenient remedy. But our object being to show how by a proper mode of life the body may be put into a state of health in which it is the least likely to need any help from drugs or special treatment, it would be clearly out of place, and imply a want of faith on our part in our present system if we thought it in the least necessary to talk much about remedial treatments. But there are certain simple applications of water and heat, which though they may be adopted remedially, are yet part of a rational and healthy mode of life—that is to say, they can both be used by anyone suffering from some definite complaint, and at the same time belong to the daily and regular *régime* of the thoroughly healthy man. The different sorts of baths, for instance, are, if rightly and scientifically used, both remedial, and will form part of the daily treatment of the healthy body.

As far as concerns the upper classes, at any rate, there is probably no race in the world which nowadays[10] uses so much water as the Anglo-Saxon; but our manner of using it is, to a large extent, luxurious rather than practical, sensuous rather than sensible. The morning cold bath, for instance, which some Frenchman the other day wittily called the "Englishman's castle," is, though eminently healthy and invigorating for some people, neither healthy nor invigorating for all, and cleansing for none except in a slight degree. The cold bath, indeed, is a sort of fetish; it is regarded as a piece of ritual belonging to the scheme of things which "makes us Englishmen what we are," and to criticise the use of cold baths is something like "taking the breeks off a Hielander." But for the sake of those thousands who have cold baths because it is their habit, and feel rather chilled and dispirited than otherwise by the process, it is perhaps worth while to say a few words about cold and other baths.

Water hot or cold, externally applied, has three main functions: (i.) to cleanse, (ii.) to promote or equalise circulation, (iii.) to invigorate and harden. It is mainly to its excellent effects with regard to the third of these functions that the complete cold plunge owes its popularity; for nothing—*given that the heart is strong, and the liver not prone to sluggishness*—is more delightfully exhilarating than the sudden thrill of cold water when one is either warm from hours in bed, or hot from violent exercise. But it must be remembered that it is distinctly not given to everyone to be sufficiently robust to be able to indulge in it. There are some people who are clearly benefited—as far as we can see—by it; there are many who are not injured by it, and can continue to take it for the sake of the pleasurable sensation it produces; but there are also many who are injured by it, who run a risk anyhow in its use. For the shock and contrast of it is a shock: a sudden drag is put on the racing heart, a sudden check is given to the hot open-pored skin. It is exactly that which is pleasant: it is that also which may be dangerous. Luckily the test of its desirability, or at any rate, harmlessness in any special case, is easy to apply, and if anyone feels chilled after cold bathing, or finds that after it the feet and hands are a little numb and cold, with perhaps a loss of colour under the nails, it is fairly certain that he or she has not the circulation which can be benefited by a cold bath; but may be hurt by it. Or if anyone finds it necessary to make a very vigorous use of the rough towel afterwards in order to get warm again, the cold bath probably does not suit him. Again, in some it produces a certain torpidity of the liver, equally easily indicated; here, also, we have one of Nature's clear danger-flags waving us off.

The cold bath suits and probably benefits most of those who do not feel these dispiriting after-effects, and the reason for it is obvious. The cold water checks the circulation momentarily; it is literally a cold sponge on the heart, and it momentarily drives away the blood from the skin. But then, if the bather has good natural reaction, this momentary chill will be succeeded by a fresh assertion of his vigour; the heart momentarily checked will, combatively, reassert itself, the blood will rush back to the skin vessels from which it has been momentarily driven, and the exhilaration of the cold shock will be succeeded by a fresh exhilaration of tingling vigour. But in any case a cold bath should not be taken by anyone already cold or chilled; it is because the body is warm, the heart beating fully, and the circulation vigorous that the subsequent reaction is vigorous. But to take a cold bath when one is cold is to demand an effort from something which should be not checked but encouraged.

As a cleanser, however, the cold bath is, we regret to say, hopelessly incompetent. For to clean the skin properly it is not sufficient to clean the mere surface of the skin. The pores have to be opened and the dirt and waste products, ordinarily invisible to the eye, taken from them. Now cold water cannot do this, since one of its main effects is to close the pores. But if anyone wants to see what happens when the pores are thoroughly opened and cleaned, let him take a Turkish bath and be well rubbed afterwards. What was ordinarily invisible becomes offensively visible, and though much of what comes away is skin itself, it is skin anyhow of a certain colour, and that colour is neither white nor pink, nor brown, but black. And the colouring matter of that is— dirt.

Now very hot water has in one respect the same immediate function as very cold water; it tightens and closes the skin, and a short very hot bath is as invigorating and bracing as a cold one, and may be used with pleasure and effect by those who are not naturally suited to the cold. But after a very short time, if one remains in a hot bath, the opposite effect begins. The heat will now open the pores of the skin, and, as the water soaks in, the skin is again relaxed, and the hot bath becomes the cleanser. For the first few moments, however, the opposite effect takes place; the skin is braced and tightened, and thus we find that many of the Japanese, for instance, and some athletes in America, use a short hot bath as we naturally use a cold bath, for an invigorator and hardener, and to close the pores of the skin. It is this use of it that we recommend to those who cannot stand a cold bath.

The hot bath, then, will supply the invigorating functions of the cold, if it is really hot and is not too long. In the same way both it and warm baths supply the cleansing functions which are wanting in the cold bath, and the combination of the two—*i.e.*, a hot or warm bath for purposes of cleansing followed by a cold douche or cold sponging, is perhaps the most perfect application of water in all its uses that we know, and contains the same principles as the Turkish bath. Those who have bathrooms will, of course, find this method easy enough to manage, but those who have not can get a perfectly adequate substitute in a large basin of cold water with which they will sponge themselves after the ordinary hip-bath or sponging-tin in their rooms and while still standing in it. Those, however, whom the cold bath does not suit, would be wise to use only cool, not cold water, after the hot bath. A further benefit of this combination of hot and cold water lies in the hardening effect which the change of temperature produces on the skin, for it accustoms it to sudden changes of temperature, and renders it far less liable to catch cold. This, in view of the number of colds that people certainly catch by getting chilled after being hot, is a great advantage.

The best, as also far the pleasantest water to wash in is soft water, approaching as nearly as possible to pure or distilled water, which from its purity and freedom from suspended mineral matter is more eager, so to speak, to take dirt, etc., into solution—that is to say, to wash it off. But distilled water is expensive; rain water, which comes nearest to it, not always to be had; while in chalky districts the water is hard. This hardness may, however, be taken off by the addition of a little oatmeal, or soda, or bath salts, which it will be found give the water the advantages of soft water; soap, for instance, lathers much more readily in it, and thus its efficiency as a cleanser is increased. Hard water also, if continually used, certainly has a sort of drying and unpleasant effect on delicate skins, making them less supple and elastic, and diminishing their power of natural healthy action. The remedy mentioned above largely alleviates this.

With regard to the third of the main functions of water—namely, to promote and equalise circulation, this effect, though obtained from a complete bath (as, for instance, a hot bath when one is chilled) is more particularly to be got from partial baths. Many people, for instance, suffer from cold feet and hands, and such know how unsatisfactory is the effect, when working, for instance, on a cold day, of warming the hands at the fire; for this relief is hardly more than momentary, and as soon as the, mere surface heat obtained is exhausted, the hands are just exactly as cold as they were before. But a remedy far more satisfactory in its effects and just as simple lies at the nearest hot and cold-water taps, and anyone who tries the effect of letting the hot water run over his hands for a few moments followed by the cold water (combining the two in exactly the same way as suggested for the complete bath, but repeating the process a few times) and then drying them thoroughly with a little friction, will quite certainly find the need of constant excursions to the fire much curtailed. For this is a warming on sound principles—the faulty circulation in the hands is remedied, the blood is stimulated to flow there naturally, and in consequence the effect is far more lasting than the momentary relief of the external heat from the blaze.

In the same way with cold feet, though it would be extravagant and foolish to recommend any busy man to put in his office a hot and a cold foot-bath, into which in the presence of his admiring clerks he should in the middle of the morning dip his feet, yet many will find the habit of cold feet greatly reduced if at the morning bath (whether they have a hot bath or a cold) they apply first hot then cold water to their feet. Again, at night cold feet are a definite and common cause of insomnia, which many unwisely remedy by heaping the bedclothes over them till they restore heat to the feet by immoderate clothing over the whole body. We have suggested in the chapter on sleep the expedient of an extra coverlet over the feet, and the hot bottle is another remedy. But there are many to whom the hot bottle is of a gruesome nature; if it is of earthenware there is the collision with the toe sometime during the night, while if it is of india-rubber there is something clammy and snail-like about it when it has grown cold. The far more thorough and satisfactory system for any confirmed sufferer, because it tends directly to improve the circulation in the feet, and to harden them by the change of temperature, is the hot foot-bath, succeeded by cold sponging and rubbing before going to bed, or after going to bed if there is insomnia. This is particularly efficacious if repeated a time or two. The tingling warmth, due to the restoration of circulation, is far more beneficial and pleasant than the unwilling haling down of the blood to the feet, as it were, by means of a hot water bottle.

In more directly remedial aspects, we may just allude to the value of wet-packs for various parts of the body, a common and excellent instance of which is a cold compress (covered with flannel) round the throat as a cure for sore throat, or cold water bandages (also covered with flannel) for local sprains or inflammations. Such things, however, border on medical questions, and though excellent and simple remedies, are of too specialised a character to be more than alluded to.

Lying half-way, as it were, between the agents of water and heat comes the Turkish bath, that solacer in the life of many city men, who but for it would undoubtedly, in the conditions under which they live, become confirmed dyspeptics. By it, in a short time, the effects which exercise has on the skin are produced; by it also, if it is followed, as it should be, by rubbing and massage, actual (though passive) exercise is obtained. Thus it counteracts to a great extent what we have before called the "acidity" of city-life, due to its general lack of exercise, and the tendency it often produces to over-eat in proportion to the exercise taken. But frequent Turkish baths, though an excellent substitute for exercise, an excellent corrective for that which advertisements elegantly call "errors of diet," and even an excellent adjunct to exercise, should be taken as a *faute de mieux*, except in the case perhaps of very corpulent people, who find it, rightly, almost essential to keep down the excess of fat. For while the heat produces about the same effect on the skin as would heat derived from physical exertion, and while massage produces about the same effect on the muscles as does physical exercise, yet the absence of fresh air in this bath is a large defect; though, it is true, it is to a certain extent compensated by the fact that the whole body is exposed to the air for a considerable time. But considered as treatment, it is artificial rather than natural; and though certainly the skin and general health of men employed in a Turkish bath as *masseurs* is in excellent condition, yet the excessive heat (excessive, that is, in respect of the temperatures that the human body seems naturally adapted to encounter) is probably in the long run somewhat trying to the system, while the cold plunge immediately after (to many the best part of the bath) is distinctly bad for those for whom cold baths are bad. But as a substitute for exercise, and a general means of health to sedentary and city-workers, it is probably the best yet contrived. Everyone, however, should rest well after it, and lie in the cooling-room for at least half an hour, since the bath itself is violent, so to speak, and demands recuperative measures, and also because after a long exposure in the hot room even the cold douche will not at once restore firmness to the skin. But with this precaution taken the bath is not only an excellent remedy for colds, but also an excellent preventive against them, by reason mainly of the hardening effect which the sudden change of the temperature produces. As a cleanser, finally, the Turkish bath is quite unrivalled.

Of late years physicians and others, both here and in other countries, notably Denmark, Germany, and America, have accepted and striven to bring within the range of practical therapeutics the incalculably health-giving and remedial power of heat and light. This subject will be touched on in another chapter in connection with the exposure of the body to the air, while part of it is too special (as, for instance, the treatment of lupus with the violet rays of the spectrum) to be more than alluded to. The principle of it all is that light is as tonic to the body of a man as it is to a plant, and that just as a plant is sickly and pale if given insufficient light, so the body if stinted in this becomes weakly and inefficient, a cellar-grown plant. Following this clue, experiment has established beyond doubt that for anæmia of certain kinds the best possible remedy is exposure to heat and light, and in Germany there is more than one sun-cure for this, the course of treatment being that patients pass hours in the sun every day with practically no clothes on. Here in England, and especially in London, such treatment is seldom possible, the two great drawbacks being lack of sun and lack of privacy[11], and in consequence artificial light has been resorted to, not as being better than sunlight, but as the best substitute for it. Here the body is exposed to a violent illumination of electric light (the eyes and head being protected), and is given a light-bath in the same way as a Turkish bath gives a purely heat bath. Incidentally, it is true, the bath of electric light is extremely hot (a temperature far above that of the ordinary Turkish bath being reached without inconvenience or danger), but the main object is to administer the tonic of light, and of that which light becomes when it has passed through the surface-skin. Of its extraordinary effects in cases of anæmia, for instance, it is outside our province to speak, but in a modified form, *i.e.*, by exposure when possible of the body to sunlight, and the constant and unvarying desirability of living in light rooms, much of its beneficial effects can be enjoyed, and should be, by everyone. Indeed, to take the long continued effect of light, not on an individual but on a race, how much of the gaiety of the southern nations may perhaps be directly due to sunshine? Certainly "a gloomy house," or "a gloomy room," is gloomy in more senses than one, for instinctively light affects the spirits; it is tonic and invigorating to body and mind alike, and ten minutes of exposure of the whole body to the sun, fantastic as it may sound, is as great a dispeller of shadows as is the sun itself.

It is with this modified form of sun-bath (not because the sun-bath, as a treatment, is anything but admirable, but because it is in treatment of disease that it is mainly used) that we have to deal. Everyone knows how invigorating it is to have only the face and hands exposed to the sun, a twentieth part of the body, that is to say, given the sun-bath, not as a medicine, but as a sustainer of general health. Multiply this by twenty then: instead of twenty minutes in the open air, expose the whole body, if possible, when dressing, to direct sun-rays by an open window; let the fresh air and the sun "have their sweet way." Sunlight, it is sadly true, is not always available, but light is better than no light, and instead of hastening to dress after the bath in the morning, throw the windows wide, and for as long as may be (though taking a feeling of chilliness as a danger signal of Nature, indicating clothes) let your body drink in light and air. If you are of imperfect circulation, get warm first by a hot-bath and exercise, but remember that as long as you are warm, there is no conceivable danger of catching cold, and that on the first hint of cold you are almost certainly in time to dress. Also the endurance of exposure increases rapidly, and endurance of exposure is one of the first requisites of serene health, of the health that no more bothers itself about danger of catching cold than the enviable slumberer spoken of in the chapter on sleep bothers himself about getting to sleep.

No wonder the sun in Greek times was the god Apollo, the young god of health and beauty, of all that keeps men young and vigorous, of all that keeps them sane and efficient. No wonder, also, that from time immemorial the sun has been worshipped as the supreme god, for from what else but his light comes growth and health? There he is every day (or at any rate on some days) marching slowly for our behoof across a beneficent heaven, and we are like children who clench their teeth when the doctor comes, rather than show their tongue, if we strive by awnings and parasols, and God knows what infamous devices, to shut out that humane physician. Gentlemen, "The Sun."

"Air and light are essential to the development of the higher forms of animal and vegetable life in full vigour and perfection. The lowest organisms—fungi and bacilli and bacteria whose office in nature appears to be to prey upon and hasten the decomposition of their superiors in the scale of life—love, like other evil things, darkness and close dwellings. Bright sunlight (the most potent and valuable of all light) and fresh air (by oxygen the portion of food used as fuel is burnt, and heat and all forms of energy evolved, and oxygen is required for the changing and removal of waste) are as inimical to them as they are beneficial to the more perfect forms above them. The action of light is known with less precision than that of oxygen. It appears, however, to be essential to the perfect formation of the red cells of the blood—its most vital constituents. Persons who are deprived of light grow pale and bloodless. Young women brought from the country as servants or shop girls, and kept in cellar kitchens or dark work-rooms, notoriously suffer in this way. Miners also are a pallid, anæmic class. The want of fresh air has something to do with the result no doubt; yet patients in a well-lighted hospital ward appear to recover more quickly, as a rule, than those in darker rooms equally well ventilated. [Compare the interesting statistics collected in St. Petersburg by Sir James Wylie.] Altogether common experience and observation confirm the conclusion which science has hardly yet formulated, that light has a powerful and favourable influence upon animal life. Human beings grow blanched just as plants do, for the want of it. And it is not a question of colour merely; vitality is seriously lowered also. This is largely felt in great towns shaded by fog and smoke-clouds. Some recent remarkable experiments have shown that the electric light exerts a favourable influence on vegetation, second only to sunlight. It is possible that it may in like manner foster animal life." Dr. W. B. Cheadle in "The Book of Health."

In addition to the experiments on vegetation, at Cornell University in America, and by Professor Siemens in England, recent experiments have shown the value of electric light in general, and of certain colour-rays in particular, in the treatment of various diseases such as gout and its sisters and cousins, nervousness, lupus, and so on. There are already several establishments in London where electric light cures are to be obtained. Dr. Forbes Winslow in his treatise on Light speaks even more emphatically than Dr. Cheadle does about the bad effects of the absence of light. He says:—

"It is a well-established fact that, as the effect of isolation from the stimulus of light, the fibrine, albumen and red blood-cells become diminished in quantity, and the serum, or watery portion of the vital fluid, augmented in volume, thus inducing a disease known as *lukaemia*, in which white instead of red blood-cells are developed. This exclusion from the sun produces the sickly, flabby, pale, anæmic condition of the face, or ex-sanguined ghost-like forms so often seen amongst those not freely exposed to air and light. The absence of these essential elements of health deteriorates by materially altering the physical composition of the blood, thus seriously prostrating the vital strength, enfeebling the nervous energy, and ultimately inducing organic changes in the structure of the heart, brain and muscular tissue."

The use of water as a means of curing disease and of preserving health was revived early in this century by Priessnitz and his many followers. In 1896 the oldest of German doctors, Professor and Privy Councillor Adolf Kussmaul, of Heidelberg, refused to sign the programme of the commissioners for medical examinations, because "of hydropathy our young doctor, when he leaves the schools, knows nothing at all." In the same year Sir Lauder Brunton, in his Summer Lectures at St. Bartholomew's, testified to the wonderful effects of the wet-sheet-pack; and the late Dr. Carpenter, Professor of Physiology in the Royal Institution, as well as Dr. Wilson and Lord Lytton, have spoken in praise of this very cheap and simple and pleasant remedy which we heartily recommend for the reader's trial. The late Sir John Forbes wrote most enthusiastically about this and other easy water treatments, which Dr. John Goodman contrasted with the treatments by drugs, stimulants, overfeeding, and so on. As a striking example we may quote his words about Diuretics (which have been among the various means recommended for reducing weight):—

"*Allopathic Diuretics.*—Squills, digitalis, nitric ether, acetate of potash, broom-tops, dandelion, mercury.

"*Hydropathic Diuretics.*—Copious water-drinking, hot-air baths, sitz-baths, wet packing, &c. No remedies act more powerfully on the kidneys without injury. Copious drinking of barley-water is good."

CHAPTER VI.

AIR AND BREATHING.

AMONG all the millions of outside agencies that go to build up and strengthen, or if improperly used to undermine, the health of the human body, there is none so constant in our environment as air. At intervals it is necessary to eat and to sleep. At intervals it is equally essential for us to have light; but the use of air goes on from birth to death; completely deprived of it only for a few minutes we die, and it is largely because breathing is so obviously and always essential, because except in definite ill-health it is completely automatic, that few people even give a thought to the question, and most would be disposed to laugh if they were told that there are different ways of breathing, some right and some wrong. Consequently, most people with the inherent perverseness of human nature use one of the wrong ways.

Observe, for instance, the way that the first hundred people you meet down any crowded thoroughfare are breathing, and you will find probably that (leaving out of the question those who are evidently out of breath) more than three quarters have their mouths open, and are breathing through them. That is the wrong way. Many of these may have a physical difficulty in getting sufficient air through the nostrils. Some have colds, perhaps, but more have over-large adenoids. Consequently if, when you have no cold at all, you find you cannot get enough air through the nostrils without effort, go straight to a doctor. But probably you can; therefore, breathe through the nostrils. For nature, who, take her all round, is a safe guide to follow, if she clearly indicates something, has provided three passages by which air may reach the lungs. One is the mouth, two are the nostrils. But the mouth (in addition to its sense of taste most conveniently placed there) has the duty of carrying food and drink to the stomach. The chances, therefore, are that the nostrils (in addition to their sense of smell, again most conveniently placed there, a sentinel to challenge the air, as it were, as the taste is a sentinel to challenge the food) were designed to give air to the lungs. And they are not ill-contrived. Witness, to take a horrible but convincing instance, the amount of soot and smuts that are prevented from reaching the lungs if we breathe through the nose during a London fog. The nostrils are a sort of filter, tortuous, averting impurities. On the other hand, many advocates of a sensible idea (as in vegetarianism and total abstinence) are their own foes when they say that only the air warmed by the longer passage is good for the lungs and makes them less liable to catch cold. The reverse is probably the case, since people with delicate lungs are cured of their delicacy or disease in the coldest possible air, if it be dry.

Anyhow, the air gets to the lungs, otherwise we die; but the lungs, which are the largest single organ in the human body and in many ways the most adaptable, have this defect, and at the same time this enormous advantage in case of disease, that a very small part of them need be used in order to supply sufficient air to the stove of combustion. We can at will (most of us do) employ the bottom part of them only, we can (with more difficulty) employ mainly the middle part, or we can with about the same difficulty employ the upper part. But since much of the health of any organ or part of the body lies in its use, for not to use an organ either passively or intentionally implies (with the only exception of those organs which are partly intended as storers of energy) its gradual atrophy, it is clearly the path of wisdom to give the lungs their proper work. For "proper work" means not exhaustion to a healthy organ but increase of strength and health. It is on the scabbarded sword that the rust grows.

In the case of men, the use of the lower part of the lungs may at once be dismissed, for it is without exception natural and habitual, whereas in many women chest-breathing, owing no doubt largely to the use of the old and unscientific corsets, is correspondingly habitual; and for men the defect lies in hardly ever, except during violent effort, when one is out of breath, using the middle and upper breathing. Roughly speaking, lower breathing is accomplished by distention of the abdominal part of the apparatus, middle breathing by distention of the part of the body between the ribs, upper breathing by inflation of the chest. In what we call a long breath, and in a yawn, the breathing is complete throughout the whole of the lungs. It is this which is worth cultivation, not only for the sake of the lungs themselves, but for the sake of the control of breathing which is often useful.

But the main point lies in the habitual use of the whole of the lungs. Take half a dozen long slow breaths, expanding the lungs to the utmost, and again completely expelling the air, and you will find by experiment that you can hold your breath for very much longer than you could do without such preparation, the reason being that you have in the blood a store of oxygen, however minute, that will carry you on for an additional number of seconds. The advantages of this are obvious in the case of great bodily exertion when the lungs have difficulty in getting enough oxygen to supply the racing heart, for if they can easily, through thorough practice, come without effort into complete use, they will be able to supply without effort a greater fund of oxygen which automatically (and God knows how) they for ever extract from the air, returning the dead air, carbonic acid gas. In other words, the man who can without effort use the whole of his lungs will keep them in a better state of health than one who from continued non-use of the middle and upper parts of them, has not maintained them in similar vigour. Such a man, also, will be far less liable to be attacked by forms of pulmonary disease than one who has half these organs in a state which corresponds to being "below par" as applied to the whole body.

Here, as in the case of other muscles, definite exercises are good for increasing the power of the lungs.

The following will be found invariably useful:—

(1) Breathe slowly in through the nostrils till the whole of the air cavity is expanded to its fullest capacity.

(2) Hold the air there from five to ten seconds.

(3) Breathe it slowly out till the whole of the air cavity is as far as possible empty.

(4) Hold it out for from five to ten seconds.

At first this exercise will be found fatiguing to the lungs and the fatigue will be manifested, if not in giddiness, in a tendency to be out of breath. By all means be out of breath, and, when the breathing is normal again, repeat the exercise, going through it half a dozen times. After a week you will find you can repeat it a dozen times or so without intermission, or the desire for intermission. During the breathing in, it will both help the lungs and encourage a greater fulness of breath to raise the arms and shoulders. They should be held in "shrugged" position while the breath is held, be allowed to drop gradually as the breath goes out, and remain utterly relaxed during the fourth part of the exercise. This exercise will be found most beneficial in enlarging the capacity of the lungs and the power of expansion of the chest, which, by the way, is a far more important thing than the actual size of the chest. The exercise may also be used with the following (see Chapter III.):—

Stand erect with the arms outstretched and hands together in front of the face. Bring the arms quickly and suddenly back until they are level with the shoulders, still at full stretch, at the same time letting the breath come suddenly and fully into the lungs. After a pause of a second or two, with the chest inflated to its utmost, bring the arms back to the original position, expelling all the breath with the same suddenness.

These two exercises, it must be repeated, are (especially for those who need them—*i.e.*, those who have not been in the habit of using the whole of the lungs) rather trying, particularly at first; on no account, therefore, strain or exhaust yourself over them. Let the facility in doing them come slowly. These, like all lung exercise, should be performed by an open window or in a room with good ventilation and as free as possible from dust, since the point is to charge the lungs thoroughly with air, which had therefore better be pure air. The open mouth may be used in these exercises, since a full draught of air has to be taken in suddenly.

But apart from actual exercises for the lungs, an even more important point is that these organs should as far as possible be given, night and day alike, a proper supply of air for their normal and automatic working; and their one and constant demand is oxygen. Considering how much there is in existence, it is wonderful how rare civilised life has contrived to make it, while builders and architects seem to adopt the uncompromising attitude of saying, "We will give you air and draughts, or no air and no draughts." Sometimes even, by an excess of diabolical humour, they manage to give one draughts and no air, and render rooms both cold and stuffy; and the continual breathing of unvivified air, of air which has been exhausted of its oxygen by the breathing of other people and not renewed by a constant fresh supply coming in, is probably responsible for as much languor and indisposition as any of the errors of diet mentioned in the previous chapter. Nor is it the least necessary that because a room is hot the air should be bad; indeed, one of the reasons why a good fire in the room is healthy is that, if there is an adequate ventilator, the fire by its burning and by the passage of the heat up the chimney induces a current of air, and though it warms a room and may make it even over-hot, yet that heated air is not nearly so enervating as the air of a cooler and ill-ventilated room. The lungs do not in the least object to be fed with even roasted air, as in a Turkish bath, any more than they dislike air of the utmost extremity of cold; what they do rebel against is being given vitiated and exhausted air. It is the quality rather than the temperature of the air we breathe which has to be considered, and many people who say they cannot stand a hot room mean not really a hot room but a stuffy one.

We have heard a good deal lately about the policy of the open door, and recommend to our readers' serious consideration the policy of the open window as much as possible by day and always at night. Unless the head of the bed is immediately by the window (and scarcely even then), it is practically impossible to catch cold when one is in bed and properly covered. To live under canvas, for instance, means to sleep almost invariably in a thorough draught. But those who have tried that delightful mode of life know that to catch cold under such circumstances is almost unknown; one is constantly wet and is usually in a draught, but one does not catch cold because these things in themselves do not produce a cold in a healthy person, and one's health in such conditions is improved, because one has enough air and probably not too much food. The air itself is tonic, strengthening; it is largely because in civilised city-life we do not have enough that we are liable to colds. The passages to the lungs, with their lining of mucous membrane, and the lungs themselves, are clogged with impurities, and weak through a mild form of starvation. Feed them. Clean them.

We do not, however, advise the ordinary city man deliberately to sit in a draught, though if that were the only plan of getting air it might be far better than his present procedure. Instead, we recommend him to look to his ventilators, and whenever he feels that the office is stuffy let him cut another or two, one low and one high; let him—and these remarks apply to all dwellers in houses—warm his offices by fires rather than hot pipes, if possible; for fires assist ventilation while they also give heat, but pipes are valueless except for heat. Furthermore, a screen of paste-board, or if light is wanted, of glass, can often be arranged so that a window may be opened without creating a draught at all; for though draughts are not, we think, so guilty in the way of cold-giving as their reputation would seem to justify, yet they are uncomfortable. But above all have windows open during sleep, that mighty friend of recuperation, when rest ought to be brought to every organ. And the natural rest to give the lungs is to supply them with plenty of pure air, so that their work is made easy for them. Nothing is commoner than long drowsiness and heaviness on waking, even after perfectly sufficient sleep, and for this nothing is more responsible than the fact that we have been breathing all night air which has been steadily deteriorating because drained of its oxygen. Let the windows be shut by all means, if you will, while you are dressing; but while sleeping, never.

Though the lungs perform the main part of the breathing, much is done also by the skin, which has this further function of continually striving to throw off those waste products and impurities of the body which rise like scum to the surface. How vastly important these functions are is shown by the story of Pietro Riario, the boy Cardinal-Archbishop of Florence, who at a feast gilded a child all over to serve as a huge lamp bearer, with the consequence that in a few hours the unfortunate victim died. It is clearly, then, desirable to listen to the demands of the skin, which are as simple and intelligible as those of the lungs, and consist of air, warmth (though to a far less extent than is generally supposed), and cleanliness. It is by clothing and baths that we meet these demands.

Now our general method of dealing with the skin is to wrap it up and put it in the dark; in other words we cover it as much as possible, because we say it is delicate and to expose it gives us colds. It is delicate—that is quite true; but what has made it delicate is our habit of covering it up. A woman, for instance, will pass with arms, shoulders, breast, and a large part of the back bare, out of a heated ball-room into a cool sitting-room and not catch cold, because her skin is used to what—as far as the skin is concerned—is most sanitary and healthy treatment. She does not catch cold, because her skin is used to it, and one of the surest ways to guard against colds is deliberately and every day to accustom it to exposure. Reasons of decency forbid us to make this a public performance, but everyone can and should adopt some course of the following kind. Strip completely on getting up and (whether the bath, hot or cold, is taken immediately or not) go through the other incidentals of dressing, shaving, etc., without clothes on. Similarly at night undress completely at once and give the skin ten minutes' airing before getting into bed. At the same time, it is well to avoid any feeling of chill, and if it is cold, sit before the fire a few minutes, or, better still (unless you find that they keep you awake), have a few minutes at the exercises given above, which will supply a more thorough and invigorating warmth. The effect of this simple treatment is, as we know from personal experience, quite amazing, both in its hardening virtues, whereby we are far less liable to catch cold at sudden chills or changes of temperature, in its tonic effect on the skin itself, as shewn in a vastly increased firmness and elasticity, and also in the constant and immediate feeling of freshness that it produces. We all know how vivifying is fresh air on the face only; here the whole skin is invigorated.

Not less important is the matter of clothing, which should be in the first place as natural as possible, so that it may not distort the natural shape, or cramp a natural movement. In the main, the ordinary man's clothing, though ugly enough, is in this respect sensible, except with regard to boots, which really seem to be an invention of the devil so as to thwart in every possible way what was meant to be the natural play of the foot. Toes in a bunch, like asparagus, tightness over the insteps, and the whole infernal contraption strapped on by a cruel string cramping the muscle above, the ankle! A more insanitary contrivance, or one better calculated to cramp the muscles and distort the shape of the foot, especially if a man take much exercise on his feet, could not be devised. Moreover, there is a sort of idea that boots which conform to the natural shape of the foot must necessarily be clumsy. This is not the case; but even if it were, it would be the part of sense to go clumsily but healthily shod. What is necessary is to be carefully measured for boots with the two feet separately, and with the *weight resting on the foot that is being measured*, since the weight naturally spreads out and flattens the foot, and it is of the first importance to have a boot that is not cramped when the muscles of the foot are being used. It is the toes that chiefly suffer in ill-fitting boots, since the boot is, as a rule, made broad enough for the foot in repose, but does not allow for the spread of the toes which takes place (or should take place) every time a step is made. At this moment it is obvious that the toes are being used as a lever to throw the body forward to its next step, the whole weight is for the moment on them, and their natural and reasonable tendency is to flatten out. Instead of allowing for this, most bootmakers make their boots for the foot in rest, with the result that the toes get crushed together at each step. This point, doubly important in the case of children whose feet are still growing is, it is satisfactory to see, being taken into serious consideration at last, and year by year more children are allowed to wear sandals, either with or without socks—an admirable institution, for they give the foot its natural development. Many women's feet are really altogether unfit for walking purposes owing to the persistent way in which they have been cramped from childhood upwards, following the barbaric and Chinese fashion of considering a small foot a beautiful thing. A delicately made foot of course is, but a foot naturally of moderate size and cramped of its growth is merely a shapeless lump of bent bones and packed flesh.

Secondly, clothing should be as easy as possible; there should not be pressure, except for definite medical purposes of support, on any part of a properly developed body; for pressure not only prevents the free flow of blood to the capillary vessels of the skin, but checks the play of any muscle which is being used, forbidding its expansion at the moment of its energy, and thus cramping the freedom of its movement.

Thirdly, clothing should be as light as is possible consistently with reasonable warmth. What is wanted, therefore, next the skin (in cold weather at any rate) is some material like wool, which is porous and therefore holds in its interstices innumerable little air-chambers that when once warmed by the heat of the body form between it and the outer clothing and air a layer of protection. It is exactly this plan that nature has adopted in the covering of birds, and we find the lower part of the feather-quill clad, not in the hard plumage of its tip, but in soft down which interposes a cushion of air between the body and the atmosphere. This is especially and markedly the case in aquatic birds, part of whose body is incessantly in water; the natural oil of the stiff part of the feathers is absolutely waterproof, while the down near their base prevents, by its air and warmth-holding capacities, the chill of the water reaching the body. Wool also has this advantage, that it absorbs moisture, and thus a man clad in under-garments of wool will be less liable to take cold if he gets chilled after violent exercise, since the sweat is to a large extent drawn away from complete contact with the skin.

On the other hand, cotton or silk next the skin, while it is less warming and has not the full protective advantages of wool, gives more air to the skin, since it does not cling so closely, and thus facilitates the breathing functions of the skin, and also allows more light to pass through it. Much must depend on the constitutional vigour of the skin in individual cases, and on its reacting powers. For a person naturally liable to catch cold, wool is certainly the safer clothing.

Finally, all clothing worn next the skin should be very frequently washed, for it is absorbing all day and every day the waste products of the skin; it should also be well aired before use and kept if possible, not in hermetically sealed drawers, but where air can get to it.

Perhaps no change of fashion in the last fifty years is greater than the change that has come over bedrooms. Fifty years ago the ordinary healthy man (if he could afford it) slept in a deep feather-bed into which his unfortunate body sank and was smothered; his bed was probably draped at the head with large curtains so as to prevent anything like a movement of air getting to him (not that it was very likely, for he kept his windows shut and curtained), while in case of anything so untoward happening he had an additional protection in the shape of a nightcap, while over the whole bed, as likely as not, was a heavy quilt. In fact, the bed gear of fifty years ago was all that bed gear should not be. By degrees the curtains were taken down, the feather mattress was supplanted by a thinner and harder affair which got its elasticity from springs below it, windows were opened, and the nightcap wore out and was not replaced. In fact, the proper rule—the utmost coolness consistent with comfort— came in. The head should be cool, the body not hot nor smothered airlessly beneath masses of coverlets. The feet, however, unless naturally warm, may with advantage have a rug thrown over them; for, if they are warm, proper circulation of the blood is ensured, and a most fruitful cause of insomnia removed.

To sum up in one sentence the general principles we have tried to lay down in this chapter, we should say, "When in doubt, open it or take it off"; the point being that you should whenever possible expose yourself to air. Think for a moment of the different *régime* adopted now, not for people in health, but for consumptives, from what those unfortunates suffered thirty years ago, and think also of the vastly increased percentage of recoveries. Thirty years ago patients were sent to warm enervating places, draughts and cold were treated as if they themselves were the microbes of disease. Now *air, air, air,* and when the damp and dulness of English winters arrives, up they go into piercing elevations of Swiss mountains. And if air will heal definite disease, we may take it completely for granted that so natural a remedy will be highly beneficial to those in health, for it must and does act as a preventive to disease, and is in itself health-giving. So also with clothing: when in doubt take it off, for the more the skin is either directly exposed or, though clad, allowed to get the maximum possible of air and light, the healthier and the more vigorous it will become; and instead of saying, "Put on a coat, or you will catch cold," it will be nearer the truth to say, "Continue not to put on a coat and you will not catch cold." Of course, there are an immense number of days when, especially if one is out in the open air without taking exercise, a coat is advisable, since the feeling of being cold is a natural danger signal, and it is then our business to get warm. But the habit of being cold is often due—and this is our point—to a relaxed and unvigorous condition of the skin, and the coat is, as it were, only a dose to meet a special need, whereas the rational treatment is to get the skin into such a condition that the body is less liable to feel cold. And this diminished liability to feel cold is promoted, not by covering the skin up, but by accustoming it to be uncovered.

CHAPTER VII.

SLEEP, REST AND RELAXATION.

THE late Sir Andrew Clark once said that he never knew anyone die from insomnia, though he knew of many who had died from trying to cure it. To a man who really suffers from insomnia, perhaps, this is but doubtful consolation, but in any case the latter half of this great doctor's remark is valuable. For probably more poison is taken to remedy insomnia, and on the whole with worse results, than in the alleviation of any other disease which flesh is heir to. Drugs, especially narcotics, are the most dangerous things in the world to play with, since so many, if taken at all continuously, almost necessitate a gradual increase in quantity. Besides, the morphia habit, or any habit of that sort, is, frankly, the clutch of the fiend, and it would be infinitely better to die of insomnia (were it possible) than be dragged down to that particular Hell.

But it is not of these martyrs, whose case is one for doctors (who will most likely be unable to help them), but of the ordinary man who may, perhaps, not be a regularly good sleeper, and of those who are habitually good sleepers, that we propose to speak. People who sleep well, and know nothing about other forms of rest, may, perhaps, find certain things here said, fantastic, but the problem of rest is just as fascinating as the problem of energy, and curious though it sounds, rest can be induced and improved even by exercises.

Broadly, then, rest and recuperation, which is equivalent to the act of gathering energy, and is necessary to the employment of it, may come in three fairly distinct ways, either by sleep, or by mere quiescence, or by intentional and definite relaxation. The two first are purely natural, being the instinctive demands of the brain and body after a period of activity; the third is, at first anyhow, an artificial rest, to be had always at command, and demanding more than mere quiescence to induce it.

To take sleep first, it should be a condition as automatic as breathing, but by its very nature, by the fact that, in order to arrive at it, both body and mind must pass into and through a quiescent state, so that the condition of unconsciousness may naturally come, it has many more foes than the mere taking and expelling of breath. A severe pain in the foot or any remote organ of the body will make sleep difficult, if not impossible, until exhaustion has come, whereas such a pain would not in any way prevent breathing; or, again, any anxiety or tension of mind will hinder sleep. Continued pain, of course, results in bodily exhaustion, continued anxiety in the corresponding exhaustion of the mind, the inability to *think* longer; but these are rather special causes of sleeplessness, which are responsible for a comparatively small percentage of those patients—for they are no less— who habitually sleep badly, either finding difficulty in getting to sleep, or awaking at timeless hours, or awaking, not to sleep again, in very early hours of the morning. These, though one can class all under the general heading of bad sleepers, are divisible into at least two distinct classes, while insomnia may arise from very different causes.

Certain general rules apply to everyone in the regulation of the bedroom, and though confirmed bad sleepers may scoff at the notion of furniture and bedgear having anything to do with their own particular thorn in the flesh, it will at any rate be harmless for them to know how a bedroom can be regulated in order to give the best possible conditions.

In the first place, then, mere stuffiness of a room will be often quite sufficient to wake an ordinarily good sleeper, and if continued, to get him into the habit of sleeping badly. If the air in a room gets exhausted of its oxygen, he will during sleep breathe through his mouth as well as his nostrils, the lungs rebelling against their starvation. This continued for several hours will by the consequent dryness of mouth and throat, and the discomfort ensuing upon it, be quite sufficient to wake him, wake him thoroughly, that is to say, with a sense of uneasiness amounting to positive discomfort. A proper bedroom, therefore, should be incapable of stuffiness, that is to say, a window should always be open, and the room be as free as possible from curtains and carpets. No doubt the absence of them (of carpet, anyhow) affects the stuffiness of a room only in a very small degree, but it has its value in this way, that the air is far freer from dust, which is an important point, if for eight hours or so out of every twenty-four you are breathing that air. But it is true that the influx of light in the early morning tends to wake some people, and the absence of curtains lets in light. For this there are two remedies, both equally simple: have blinds of the ordinary dark-blue stuff which quite effectually excludes light, or better, pass a couple of nights, three or four perhaps, in which you are awakened by light. After that you will fail to notice it, and one of the present writers, who for years thought he must awake when light came in, found after doing so once only, that it made not the slightest difference, and he who carefully drew curtains, and had the position of a strange bed altered so as to be away from the light has now often awoke, when called, in a blaze of sunshine.

He is, therefore, you will conjecture, a naturally good sleeper. Naturally, no—that is to say, in early life he was a persistently bad one, who used to adopt all kinds of means to go to sleep, of which presently. But for the last six years his record is this: he has, as far as he remembers, through good and ill report, through such anxieties as are inseparable from life itself, through one attack of typhoid fever, and two of influenza, in spite of hard work up till the time of going to bed (in fact, particularly then, since he finds he works best when the small hours begin to grow bigger), lain awake for never more than one complete hour on three occasions. Once he had coincidently a bad cold, on the other two occasions he failed then, and fails now to account for so extraordinary a proceeding. All told, then, in six years he has been awake for three solid hours when he meant to be asleep. Otherwise, he extinguishes his light—and is called.

Now the secret of this is, as far as he knows, the complete conviction that he is going to sleep, a conviction not expressed at all, but an acquired instinct. Yet he does not—he says all this at the risk of being accused of egotism, but hoping it may be useful—bother about the matter at all. Once he used to bother about it: that was in the days when he slept rather badly; now he does not. Nor does he go to bed in the hopes of going to sleep; he does not go to bed till he feels, instinctively again, that it is time. Thirdly, if he has gone to bed early, and is not going to be called till after he has had his fill of sleep (this is rare, since he is a glutton at it), he instantly reads or gets up instead of trying to go to sleep again (which in itself would do no harm), or instead of wondering why he has awoke. This would do harm, for it partakes of the nature of "bothering about it." He avoids sleep during the day, this also he thinks is crucial, and if he feels sleepy (sleepy, not to be compared with inclined to rest) he gets up and does something.

To return for a moment to his bedroom. The windows are open, there is no carpet, he has blankets which vary according to the time of year, but whatever the time of year he has an extra thickness over his feet. In his rare moments of semi-consciousness he sometimes (this is towards morning, always when the world is coldest) draws the extra covering over him, and without really waking sleeps again. He also invariably goes to sleep on his right side and invariably wakes lying on his left.

We have spoken about this enviable slumberer at some length, because he seems instinctively to have got hold of (no credit to him) some of the points which will be of use to the moderately bad sleeper, whose condition, we maintain, is wrong. If sleep is required, it is as pitiable not to get it as not to be able to eat without indigestion when hungry; if sleep is not required, it is as foolish to try to induce it as to eat when one is not hungry, also with indigestion. But to draw the lesson from this enviable slumberer, though much that he does would murder sleep like Macbeth (witness his odious habit of working immediately before going to bed), still much that he does is sensible. Pre-eminently sensible, for instance, is his acquired habit of not bothering about it, for the wondering whether one is going to go to sleep is in many cases quite sufficient to keep one awake. Go to bed assuming naturally, not with insistence, for that would spoil it all, that you *are* going to sleep, or to use a phrase from hypnotism, make the suggestion that you are. You will not succeed in capturing this attitude the first time you try, nor yet the second, but before long you probably will; probably, also, when you have done so, you will become a good sleeper. But if this fails, what then? You will lie awake, that is all, and you will not die of it. But if you fret about it you will lose all the benefit of the act of resting, which is very great. To lie still with twitching nerves, agonising for sleep, will not only not bring sleep, but it will deprive you of rest. You lie awake. Be it so—at any rate, rest.

Here innumerable complications enter. You may think it is a noise that is keeping you awake. Someone, who ought to be in bed, is moving about directly above you. Do not get irritated and think over the biting things you will say to-morrow. The morrow will take care of itself. Supposing there was a gale blowing, you would acquiesce in the Natural Law, and in consequence would go to sleep sooner, because you were not irritated. And irritation, it must be remembered, should be wholly within our control; in this case to get it in control is an essential preliminary to sleep. While you are cross you will not sleep. Therefore, cease to be cross. A greater distraction would calm your irritation; let the desire for calmness calm it.

Of great mental anxiety as a cause of insomnia, or of great physical pain, it is not our purpose to speak, for these are exceptional cases. But the ordinary person must, with an effort—until the act becomes automatic—put out of his mind when he goes to bed all interesting things, if he wishes to become a good sleeper. He must, at first anyhow, having definitely told himself that he is going to sleep, consciously let his mind dwell on monotonous affairs. Sheep going through a gap in a hedge is a recognised soporific, and no doubt an excellent one, only he must be absorbed not in each sheep but in the stupifying multitude of them. Similarly he may try to mark out a lawn-tennis court with as few possible liftings of the marking machine, without of course going over any line twice. Or he may say over and over again some passage of poetry, or some familiar form of words, which should be short, so as to procure the benefit of the tedious effect of mere senseless repetition. But, after he has wasted time—for these things are waste of time if one wants to go to sleep—in this manner, he must take into consideration methods even more simple than these. Cold feet, the least feeling of hunger will easily, especially in a nervous person, induce sleeplessness. If such causes are present, then additional covering, and some easily digestible food—biscuits, fruit, etc., will probably relieve him. Again, washing the face in cold water, also an awakening process, tends to send the blood anywhere but to the brain, which is desirable. A hot-water bottle to the feet serves the same object. Or again, failure of digestion is a common cause of sleeplessness; if there is a chance of this being the cause, drink hot water before going to bed, or cold water with a little bi-carbonate of potash.

Considering the incalculable benefit which a habit of sleep produces, we do not feel ashamed to write down aids, however tiny, to produce it. For that it is largely a habit is beyond question, and as a habit it is one of the entirely healthful habits—it is essentially good. But the contrary habit, that of lying awake, though largely remediable, is not fatal, and its ill-effects are immeasurably neutralized if the will is steadily exerted towards the grasp of that truth. To lie awake, fretting that one cannot go to sleep, is distinctly bad; to lie awake, if no remedy short of drug-drinking will cure it, does not appreciably matter, so long as one accepts "rest" as the best possible substitute.

A different variety of sleeplessness is that which attacks the sufferer early in the morning, say three or four hours before he wishes to get up. For this a somewhat heroic remedy may be tried, since it is always possible that natural awaking may mean one thing—namely, that you have had enough sleep. Therefore, it may be worth while, just once or twice, to try the effect, if you are really broad awake, of getting up instead of encouraging yourself to wake early again by letting this early waking dwell on your mind. You will probably be very tired by the next evening, you may even (in this case the remedy is clearly futile) be too tired to sleep. But it may easily happen that you will sleep that night exceedingly well, and wake at a normal time again. But if again, and yet again you continue to wake early, it is no use persisting in this treatment. Or you may awake, as stated before, owing to the airlessness of your room, and the fact that you have been breathing with an open mouth, or, and this is probably a frequent cause of early awakings, you may be engaged for weeks or months together on some absorbing occupation. You sleep at first because tired, and sleep deeply, but as the hours go by the sleep becomes lighter, and before your body regains consciousness at all, that strange part of the brain, the subliminal self, or the sub-conscious self, is awake, and begins thinking (gradually arousing the rest of you) of the engrossing occupation. Soon the whole brain is awake, and by the sub-conscious self is reminded, as it were, of the business. Then having once begun thinking about it, it is difficult for you to regain that passivity which is invariably the prelude to sleep, though it need be scarcely more than instantaneous.

It is here that the cause of sleeplessness and its remedy we believe largely lie, for it is within the power of all to put themselves into the control, more or less complete, of their sub-conscious self and develop the power of the sub-conscious self until it becomes a real potency. To take an example, how constantly does it happen that after wrestling with some mental difficulty, or trying to remember some name which one knows well, one by instinct dismisses the subject, to find in a few minutes that the difficulty is solved, or the name recollected. That is probably the work of the sub-conscious part of the brain. In the same way many people can wake themselves at any hour they wish, by telling their sub-conscious brain (this is what it comes to) to call them. They go to sleep, having ordered their sub-conscious self to call them, and at the appointed hour, it may be long before light, something inside them, which apparently knows the time, wakes the rest of the sleeping brain and body. And with a little training and practice the power of developing and using the sub-conscious brain increases very quickly. We believe that many early wakers could sleep comfortably on, by saying that they would *not* awake till a certain hour. One does not need violence or internal shouting, as it were, to communicate effectually with this sub-conscious self; a quiet determination of thought for a few moments before going to sleep does the work effectually. This also is invaluable to many who have found that going to sleep when getting into bed was difficult. One has to take it for granted that one is going to sleep, and cease to think about it, emptying the brain of conscious thought as far as may be. You cannot go to sleep in a rage, until the rage has given place to exhaustion.

To sum up, then, both for those who find it difficult to go to sleep, and for those who wake early, the following hints are recommended:—

(i.) Do not load your brain with interesting stuff, just before going to bed. This will both prevent your going to sleep, and will also tend to wake you up. Try reading a stupid book for a few minutes after getting into bed.

(ii.) Have as much air as possible in the room, and wear the minimum of bed-clothing that keeps you warm. But have an extra rug over the feet, which you can easily draw over you towards morning, when both the night is coldest, and your vitality lowest.

(iii.) If you still lie awake, try the effect of some monotonous exercise, like counting sheep going through a gap, marking out a tennis-court, or repeating some short and familiar form of words.

(iv.) If you suspect even slight indigestion, take a little bi-carbonate of soda or of potash.

(v.) Tell yourself quite quietly that you *are* going to sleep, but do not rouse yourself to see how you are getting on.

(vi.) Eat or drink something easily digestible, rice, biscuits, or hot cocoa.

(vii.) If all these are useless, be quite resigned; try not to get irritated, do not toss about if you can avoid it. Do not think about interesting things. In fact, if you cannot sleep, take as much rest as you can. Lie utterly relaxed and breathe deep. Finally, with regard to the number of hours of sleep required, it must remain a personal question. Some people do not need more than between five or six, especially in later life, others seem positively to need not less than eight. But the chances are that everyone requires from about

five and a half to eight. Less than that minimum
is probably insufficient in the long run, more
than eight probably unnecessary for anyone in
good health. Nor must it be forgotten that in
itself the desire for much sleep is not a healthy
sign; it may easily point to a sluggish liver.

This brings us to the second division of the subject—
namely Rest, which does not only largely diminish the ill-
results of not sleeping at night, but is probably good for all
hard workers either of mind or body, at certain times during
the day, in particular after a long continued stretch of brain-
work, when an interval should be taken by the mind; after a
meal, when quiescence on the part of the body leaves the
digestion more energy to do its work; and after physical
exercise, when those limbs which have borne the brunt of it
should be left quiescent. A flat or semi-recumbent position
is the best, one in which the body is completely supported,
and no muscular effort is needed to retain it in its position;
and the deep breathing of sleep may be at first imitated and
will soon be acquired. The reason for this is that since slow,
long breath is the means naturally adopted by the lungs in
sleep, it is probably the best method of resting the breathing
muscles even when awake. It is a mistake to spend too long
over these rests; if two a day are taken, a quarter of an hour,
provided it be real rest, is likely to be sufficient to freshen
one up again completely, while if the muscles are left too
long relaxed, they will be disinclined to begin work again.

Now sleep and rest are widely different from relaxation,
the third means of recuperation mentioned above, since the
first two are purely natural, and require merely passivity as
a condition, whereas intentional relaxation is at first purely
artificial, and requires, even when it has become easy with

practice, certain voluntary efforts. It has therefore this initial disadvantage, and in addition this further one, that in the young it is seldom if ever required, since the natural means of recuperation, Sleep and Rest, supply all that is wanted. Unless habits are acquired in childhood or youth, however, there are few people who will ever spare the time to acquire them at all. It requires also an exercise of imagination—rest, that is to say, has to be attained self-consciously.

This all sounds confusing, and with a view to making it rather more intelligible by an easy instance of it, the following is recommended. It is of no use merely reading it, the thing has to be tried, and after two or three trials it will be time enough to say whether the particular individual finds it of value. Thus:—

Sit straight in any chair with a back to it. Close the eyes and draw a long, slow breath in, gradually lifting up the head, and thinking as far as may be of nothing whatever. Then breathe slowly out, letting the head drop forwards and the body and spine bend forwards, till the whole attitude is that of something broken or lifeless. Repeat.

Now this may sound like a meaningless formula to any who have never tried it. But the fact remains that many who have, find—whether it is the imagination that tells them so, or not—that they gain more recuperation from a couple of minutes of this, than they possibly could in the same time-limit of mere rest or sleep. The reason is not far too seek: in sleep and in rest the muscles certainly *do* rest, but is it not more than possible that a muscle bidden by the will to rest, rests far more completely? Certainly each of the present writers, if, for instance, he is thoroughly tired, and by the exigencies of life he has to do something else in three minutes by the clock, does not attempt to lie down or go to sleep for three minutes, which he can easily do, but has found by experience that voluntary and intentional relaxation like this, dictated by the will, is far more freshening than either rest or sleep. At any rate he so believes it is, that the illusion is complete. The fact of saying to the muscles, "I *will* rest," is indeed more immediately productive of refreshment than passive rest. This may sound fantastic, but to take a larger instance, how often has it happened that a patient in some serious fever, when exhaustion is the foe to be dreaded, has pulled through by an exercise of will, by making an effort, whereas if he had lain passive—in the natural condition for recovery—he would certainly have died? There are few doctors who would not endorse this. And voluntary relaxation, in the same way, is the remedy for milder exhaustion, especially when another business has to be gone about almost immediately. To some, the note "quack" will sound here. But "quack" is worth trying, if it can do no harm.

The same exercise—one of the present writers has not personally found it so successful—may be tried standing, or in a more elaborate form, it can be tried lying. From a kneeling position on the floor, with the head forward on the chest, and the spine relaxed, one slowly, but with the vivid idea of *rest* in one's mind, crumbles down to a lying position, eventually resting on the back, with legs and arms outstretched and separate. The breathing must be full, slow, and rhythmical. Then after a minute or two one rises very quietly.

Or, again, relaxation in a milder form can hardly fail to be useful to everybody, and many people practise it unconsciously. The commonest form which is known to everyone is *stretching* at the end of work, and for a few seconds afterwards remaining utterly relaxed. No one has ever stretched—we boldly assert this—without the subsequent relaxation, which, quite apart from the relief of a cramped position that stretching gives, gives rest to the body. Similarly, also, every sedentary brain-worker will find that he works best when he is most unconscious of his body, when the energy which would be employed in bracing limbs is left unoccupied for the brain to make use of. Mere stillness is of course not at all the same thing, for stillness may go with rigid stiffness. But the point of relaxation is that during work every muscle that is not employed in that work should have nothing whatever to do, and that after work no muscle should have anything to do if the work has been physical, and if mental that the brain should be empty. True the will has to say, "Holiday for all, holiday for all," because all rest better so; but no more. *The energy of the whole frame is devoted to rest.*

In the same way, just as when the brain bears the stress of exertion, the body should be completely relaxed, so when one part of the body, the arms or legs, for instance, are actively employed, and above all when storage of energy may be useful, the rest of the body not wanted should be trained to give no trouble, not to require the usage of energy. Innumerable instances of the truth of this present themselves, for in athletics "reserve," "quietness of action," all imply the unconscious storage of energy. Force employed is energy gone, and the less unnecessary energy one spends, the more there is left for endurance. Look at a practised racket player and one who does not know how to husband himself! The one takes two quiet steps and is in easy time, the other rushes to the corner, is there before there is any need, and has to make a call on his muscles to check himself. Result, one has expended no energy, practically speaking, in getting there, the other has parted with energy twice, once to start with violence, once to check himself with violence.

This repeated twice a minute for half-an hour will leave one fresh, the other beaten.

Here we have an instance of intentional sparing, a thing related to relaxation, for both are an economy of force. And in this body of ours, so "fearfully and wonderfully made," servant as it is or should be to the will, a conscious command is far more binding than a *laisser aller*. A man with a severe headache may be unable to go to sleep in the ordinary course, but let him learn to know and practise the use of the huge power of will that is lying chiefly dormant within him, and he will not only be able to get on satisfactorily with his work, which would be impossible if he paused to think how his head hurt, but he will easily be able to go to sleep. He could, and the ordinary man can, if he tries, induce by practice both energy and passivity.

But there are "foes of its own household" even here, as in Vegetarianism and Teetotalism. And the hearth-abiding foe of the power of the will is Christian Science. This strange sect holds that *all* ailments are imaginary, and that since there is no matter, there is no such thing as a broken leg, because there is no leg. This is futile, and the answer incontestably is that there must be legs because they can be broken. But the subject is not worth discussion.

Again, to sum up:—

(i.) To mean to do a thing is productive of better
results than to let the thing happen.

(ii.) Therefore, let your will intend rest, and you will
get rest more effectively than by lying down.

(iii.) You do not tire the will by using it. On the
       contrary, it is only by its use that it can get strong.

(iv.) There are two things that weaken the will: the
      first is not using it, the second is not obeying it.

CHAPTER VIII.

THE INFLUENCE OF TRAINING ON MIND AND MORALS.

IT is impossible to make the simplest movement of any kind without the conscious or unconscious direction of the mind, so inextricably are the two bound up together; and from the earliest times physicians, both spiritual, mental and physical, have known that the soul can be reached through the "subtle gateways of the body." This aspect of training, the importance, that is, of the cleanly health of the body, and its prompt and unrebellious obedience to the will, which is concerned with this question, has been alluded to before, and is dealt with more fully here.

In the chapter on exercises we insisted that both for their direct use in athletics, and for their far greater significance in life, the speed and promptitude of the body's obedience was an attainment of great value, for thus the mind has at its call a quick ready servant to do its errands, instead of a slow loiterer. We saw, also, that these exercises, while they are in progress, necessitate strict attention, which we may now add should be consciously applied, as learnt there, to other pursuits. Let, for instance, the man who has accustomed himself by this drill, for so we may call it, to attend with concentrated attention to these simple actions of the body, apply that attitude of mind which is now familiar to him to other tasks. Let us say he has before him a tedious piece of work, which at the same time requires minute attention. Let him, then, put himself into that frame of mind (he remembers it quite well) with which he performs his exercises. Many people hardly know what real attention means: there is no better way to teach it than to make rapid and correct movements, which cannot be made without it. In the same way, also, these exercises give the habit of control. A man who has brought mind and body into the relation of master and willing servant, even in so elementary a matter as this, is going on the right road to teach himself control in the largest choices and difficulties. So, too, in other points of training: a man who has made himself able to drop smoking, or abstain from stimulants, or from certain sorts of food which he likes, but which his reason tells him are bad for him, has not improved his power of self-control in that point only, but has begun, at any rate, to form a habit of it; and the exercise of self-control, in one point only, will make his power of control stronger all round, in each and every case where his reason suggests control to him. It is here, as a tonic to the mind, that training of some sort, apart from all its other uses, is recommended to everybody; not training for some special event, which, as soon as the event has come off is dropped, but a daily and continual observance of certain rules of health, a daily practise of exertion of will and obedience of body.[12]

Again, the health of the body contributes directly to the power and strength of the mind. Work, which is irksome and comparatively badly done by a man who, for any cause, digestive or otherwise, is in only moderate health, will be done by the same man with zest and far better results if he is in good health. Also, the mind is able to accomplish not only better work but more work, when the whole system is not laid under a general tax to repair and make well any enfeebled or clogged organ. A single rusty joint, a badly fitting valve in an engine, makes the whole run less smoothly than it should, and also implies a waste of energy. Body and mind together, working in co-operation as they always must, are a close parallel to this. The one cannot possibly be at its best unless the other is in health. Rightful activity in the one stimulates activity in the other, just as artificial stimulants, such as spirits to the body, induce a mental activity in all respects like the physical one, temporary in character and followed by reaction. But the habit of briskness, of activity, of quick decision, is a thing fully as much mental as it is bodily; the two are inseparable, and, therefore, in the training of the body, the qualities which we should aim to acquire are those which are mentally desirable. One man's mind may, it is true, be naturally a much less fine instrument on its own level than his body, and much less easily trained, but the self-control, the alertness, the habit of speed, which such training as we have sketched out gives, will directly and inevitably affect his mind. It may still be slow and laborious in its workings, but it would otherwise have been slower. Also, whatever work it does it does better, because it is not clogged, hindered, and distracted by an unhealthy body.

Now this interweaving of mind and body is so complex, so closely knit, that it would perhaps be beyond the sphere of safety to say that the knitting together of the body and that within us which is the spring of moral, not intellectual qualities, the soul in fact, is closer than that of the mind and body. In any case, the interdependence of body on soul, of soul on body, and of both on the mind is practically complete, and this human trinity makes up man. There is no healthful habit of body which does not directly exercise a healthful influence on the soul, no harmful habit which does not hurt it. The body sins, and in its secret place the soul sickens. From the other side, also, a high moral standard infallibly leads the body to adopt healthy habits, a low moral standard suffers it to drift into physical crime and degradation.

Now city life, especially to anyone who has been accustomed to have a good deal of exercise without a modification of the food and stimulants he may take without hurt in a more active country life, is apt to put the body into a state which renders it particularly liable to all kinds of moral attack. The life is largely sedentary, and in consequence a great deal of physical vigour in young men, which would in the country be naturally and healthily expended in games and exercise for the upper classes, in manual labour for the lower, remains unused, and, except to those of strong moral principle, is a dangerous thing. Again, without modification of diet to suit the circumstances, most people eat more stimulating food than they require, and, as a natural sequence, drink more stimulating and intoxicating drinks than are good for them. This, in itself, is another exciting cause to the passions. To exercise self-control under these circumstances is a laudable and a difficult thing; but a far simpler remedy lies to hand—namely, in not letting these circumstances exist, by deliberately taking less stimulant and deliberately stinting oneself in the matter of food, or giving a fair trial to the simpler foods spoken of before, which will be found to be far less exciting, though quite as nourishing. There are many men who are capable, as far as will power goes, of limiting themselves in this manner, who, if they do not limit themselves, become nearly helpless in the grip of their temperament. For a life of sensual indulgence, to put it on the lowest grounds, is bad for the body and the mind; sensual thought even becomes a habit as hard to get rid of as any morphia habit, and for many to try to rid themselves of it, while they continue to keep their bodies in a permanent state of excitability owing to overmuch food and stimulant, would be like attempting to cure the morphia habit, and yet continually going about with a phial of it in the pocket. And nothing, again putting the question on low grounds, is so bad for the nerves as to be incessantly desiring and dwelling in thought upon a certain thing, and incessantly refusing to gratify the desire. We do not, of course, mean that it would be better to gratify it,' but that it is better to take hold of it by the root, not merely pinch the stem, and, as far as possible, get rid of the desire. For there are certain temptations, and impurity is one, which are not safe to fight consciously, since to approach them even in thought means to be seized, as it were, by the tentacles of some infernal cuttlefish. Do not school yourself to fight them; school yourself to run away from them. Interest yourself in other things, tire yourself physically, and, above all, do not indulge in stimulants of food and drink, which, however innocent they may be in themselves, predispose, by the very feeling of vigour they give, to things which are not innocent.

It is not only the suddenness and almost overwhelming force of physical temptation to some natures which constitutes their only danger, it is the gradual, hardly observable nature of the effect of such indulgence. For years, it is no use denying it, a man's mental and bodily health may continue, as far as one can see, absolutely unimpaired by such excesses. The greatest harm is done by preachers, schoolmasters, and others who warn boys that such habits will lead to immediate decay of the mental and physical powers, and early death. The boy may be frightened for a time, but if this is the only preventive that keeps him back, his fright will wear off, and he will find by experience that no such effect, as was predicted, follows. He will, therefore, probably conclude that there is no ill-effect. He will, also, assuredly meet men who tell him that such practises are good for the health. A greater fallacy was never invented by the devil himself. There is no truth whatever in it. But what his teacher ought to have taught him was that such practices are the cause of mental and physical decay in thousands, though not immediately, that to yield to such temptations is for everyone to become less able to resist them, and that by perfectly simple rules in the use of water, in the limiting of food especially, for instance, late in the evening the force of such temptations becomes infinitely less. Many people, no doubt, will say that this is a low ground on which to build up high motives. It is for that very reason, since it will appeal to those to whom high motives would not appeal, that it is so extremely useful. Thus it will appeal to many to know that at the age, let us say, of fifty, a man who has lived purely is, almost without exception, a stronger and more vigorous person, more capable of work and also of enjoyment than one who, in early manhood has, though possibly for a few months or weeks only, behaved like a mere 'brute beast.'

It is in this connection that we strongly advocate the introduction into London and other big towns of those evening clubs for exercise, which have been tried with great success in America. There are boys' and men's clubs in enormous numbers in London, and admirable things they are, but we know of few where billiards is not, perhaps, the most violent form of exercise provided. What is wanted is a number of tall buildings built with many floors, where, for a moderate subscription, that class of young man who now spends his evenings in the promenade of the music halls, or in aimless (perhaps it would be better if they were aimless) strolls up and down Piccadilly with not infrequent visits to the public house, could get an hour's violent exercise in boxing, fencing, or gymnastics. We fully believe that this class, as a whole, would enjoy such an evening far more than the evenings they are now accustomed to spend; that it would be infinitely better for them in body, mind and soul alike, not even the flabbiest moralist would be disposed to deny. As it is, a young man gets away from his work, say at five or so, and what in heaven's name is the poor vigorous thing to do with the hours that divide him from his natural bedtime?[13] It is out of the question to expect that he should sit in his room and read a book; he has been at work all day; his body tingles for diversion. Out he goes, if he is human at all. In the general way there are two places open to him, the public-house or the streets. There his vigour finds further stimulus, or unhappily, its satisfaction. That there are, as we have said, many clubs for such people is perfectly true, but papers, draughts, chess (and we suppose now pingpong), are not the sort of thing that is needed to work off the potential violence of the body. What is wanted is violent exercise.[14] That such institutions would be enormously popular with the class of which we speak, those, in fact, for whom more expensive clubs are utterly out of the question, is, we think, beyond doubt, and financially, we believe, that they could quite easily be made to pay. It would, of course, be out of place to discuss this here, but it is worth noting that where such clubs have been tried in Boston and elsewhere, they have proved successful.

It is these evening hours which are the dangerous time. Purposeless loafing in the streets, though entertaining enough, is not sufficient for a vigorous young body, which has been pent all day at work; while loafing with purpose, we may say, is not good for anybody, yet it is to loafing with purpose that purposeless loafing naturally leads. Purposeless loafing is innocent enough, but, to use the morphia simile again, it is as if the sufferer from the morphia habit took a bottle of morphia and continued to finger it, a highly dangerous performance; and we do not believe that the class which loafs in the streets, anyhow the best of them, loaf because they prefer it to some suitable employment for their body, but because no suitable employment for their body, is accessible to them. The bulk of them would vastly prefer something different, and the eagerness with which they would embrace bodily exercise may be gathered from the crowds on the Serpentine and waters of the park if skating is possible. The theatre every night is, of course, as hopelessly out of their means, as it would be to belong to Prince's or Lord's, but with what patience and in what numbers do the crowds wait at the pit door. The middle classes of England, we believe, are not naturally sensual, but, as it is, during just those hours in the day when they are at leisure, there is nothing whatever for them to do, except loaf, till loafing becomes a habit, and from being an innocent one passes into the Devil's care, who has made the London streets what they are, down the most populous of which, Piccadilly, the Strand, etc., no man would willingly take his sister at night.

It is towards this removal of causes that predispose towards ill-health in the moral sphere, ill-health as shown by a lack of energy, promptitude, power of work and endurance in the mind, that the training of the body, as we have attempted to outline it, is largely and unceasingly devoted. Health, as we understand it, the condition, that is to say, not of the ordinary man who considers he is "well enough," but that higher health which is the result of training the body to quickness, energy, and so to strength, which implies an obedience to the reason in matters of food and stimulants, directly benefits a man's moral and mental life. The body "is in subjection"; it obeys with less struggle the dictates of the non-material part of man, and it obtains in itself a greater resistive power to temptations of laziness or lust, just as it obtains a greater resistive power to its own purely physical enemies of cold or fatigue. It is in this respect, therefore, (a far higher consideration than mere physical fitness), that we put forward a system of training that will be likely to ensure such results, and that consequently we regard the obedience to laws of bodily health, and means of physical fitness, as partaking of the nature of duty. And this further: it is clearly accepted as man's duty that he should keep his mind and his morals in the highest and best possible state; but seeing how intimately both these are knit with his body so that none can act without the other, the soul sinning through the body, the mind dictating every movement, is it reasonable to suppose that a corresponding duty is not laid on man with regard to the health of his body? Is it not, in fact, directly his duty to keep his body, as well as his soul and mind, in its highest and best possible state? No doubt compromises have often to be made; a man, in order to do his work, may be obliged to disregard certain rules which the health of his body requires should be kept. But saving this, there seems to us to be a clear duty with regard to physical health, quite apart from the advantage which physical health will bring to his mind and morals. This wonderful machine is a servant, no doubt, of the mind, but shall the master keep it, so to speak, in an insanitary attic, and pay no regard to its health? The compromises also, which we have just spoken of, will be rarer if the body is well, since it will be more capable of bearing fatigue and unreasonable hours of work.

The simple, but unswerving principles on which morals are based, the highest development of the mind, the utmost health of the body: these things, and nothing short of them, are the results of ideal training.

CHAPTER IX.

TRAINING FOR SPECIAL EVENTS.

THE excuse for this chapter in a book written (as set forth), not for the athlete primarily, but for the average man, who is hopelessly incapable of prominence or great excellence in any one branch of athletics, lies in the fact that such a vast number of people nowadays play games, and are so anxious on certain days to do their best at them in some competition, that quite a fair percentage of readers will, it is hoped, pick up a hint or two which may serve them in good stead at that trying moment when they are about to drive a ball from the first tee on some medal day; about to step out on to the glaring prominence of a lawn-tennis court; about to go in (fifth wicket down) when a rot has apparently set in; or, may be, to play a preliminary tie in the City and Suburban Ping-pong Handicap. For it is at these cold and shuddering moments, which no one can hope to meet with more than stolidity, that one needs to have all one's wits about one, to be able to keep one's nerve, and to have one's strong points at one's fingers' ends, and one's weak points (we all have these, and the better one grows at any particular sport, the more glaring they seem proportionately to become) anyhow passably defended. At one minute, or less, from now it may be that your weak point will be attacked; your drive may land you a full iron shot from the green, a stroke you particularly detest; you may have a scurry after a cross-court return; you may have a yorker on the leg stump. In all such, the important thing is, not only to be prepared for them now, but to have been prepared for them so long before that the preparation has become a habit. Such strokes may still be your weak point, but you will meet the emergencies calmly.

And to meet any emergency calmly is in itself a favourable defence, for you will then no longer be flurried.

Now in any game, when you have to meet a definite attack of an opponent—this necessity does not apply to a game like golf, or croquet, or billiards, since in such games you have to do the best you can yourself, without fear of active opposition—there is a golden rule, which has never been enough insisted on, and it is the rule that lies at the base of all we have said about training generally, as applied to games. Practice is at the root of it, and the object is to get so familiar with the stroke dictated by the exigencies of the moment, that it is practically automatic.[15] That is to say, as soon as the attack (your opponent's return, or the bowler's ball) is coming, you will, with the least possible expenditure of energy, recognise it, get into the position to meet it, and have the stroke ready. For instance, if the game is lawn-tennis, you will see that a drive into the left-hand corner of the court is probable, and before you have really formulated this to yourself consciously, you should be half-way there, not vaguely, but ready for the attack. Your body should have moved almost automatically, and thus your attention and will-power is reserved for noticing your opponent. He may change his mind at the last second (you can never tell about opponents), and instead of driving into the left-hand corner he may lob gently over the net into the right-hand court. Thus your attention, which would—had you not cultivated a sort of correct automatonism—have been used up in getting into the left-hand corner, will be free to observe his change of tactics, and the result is that you will be far more ready for his new attack than you would have been, if all your attention had been taken up in getting into position yourself.

This verbose illustration is necessary to explain a thing that is often overlooked—namely, the necessity of observing your opponent; and the more automatic your own preparations are, and the more instinctively the body works,[16] the more attention you have at your disposal. It follows, as a corollary, that the less trouble you have to take to meet the actual attack, the more you can concentrate your mind on your opponent. The eye should send to the brain the message—"Yorker on the leg stump," or whatever it may be—and with *the least possible expenditure of force, either of muscle or nerve*, the attack should be met. The more the movements of the body are automatic, the less you will exhaust yourself. This, in a hard-fought game of racquets, for instance, is an incalculable advantage.

But in order to ensure this automatic movement there is one thing absolutely essential, and that is not practice merely, but correct practice and swift practice. And correct swift practice implies not only much repetition, but concentration of mind. If you perform a new movement a hundred times, let us say, without thought, it may be done correctly, but it cannot be done, if correctly, swiftly. Correctness is the first essential, as we said in the chapter on exercise, and always essential; the swiftness in execution comes mainly with practice; so also does the automatic performance of the correct movement. But it is a very easy thing to lose correctness as the speed increases, and with a view to right this we have recommended—after the movement has been completely understood, and learned in some cases part by part—practice before a glass.

This, then, is the first essential—namely, to have practised one's weak points till, though they are still perhaps weak, they are performed with the minimum possible of conscious thought, so that one's attention, as far as may be, is free to observe the opponent. For a long time before the match continually practise your weak points, till they become, if not satisfactory, at any rate fairly easy, and give to your strong points only that amount of practice which will serve to keep them in repair, so to speak. At the time of the event, of course, you will use them as much as you possibly can, and at the same time give your opponent as few chances as possible of attacking your weaknesses. And the knowledge that you have a passable defence for such weaknesses, and can use it with moderate ease, will vastly increase your measure of confidence, whereas the knowledge that in some one point or so you are nearly defenceless would cramp and worry you throughout the set.

Again, since in many cases correctness of striking lies between two opposite faults, it is often useful to practise deliberately the fault which is opposite to your besetting sin. If, for instance, you do not use your wrist enough in a certain stroke, practise using it far more than is in the least advisable; if, on the other hand, you use it too much, not giving the forearm, for instance, its share in the stroke, practise the stroke with the forearm alone, keeping the wrist rigid, and you will often find that you thus attain correctness more quickly than if you had practised correctness. The longest way round, in fact, is here the shortest way home.

It is a great fallacy, as we have said before, to suppose that mere practice makes perfect. Instead of improving, you may be merely ingraining an existing fault; or, again, practice without briskness and without full attention given is only practice in sluggishness, and confirms and strengthens want of concentration. Thus it is always better, if possible, to practise in short spells, and never go on if you find your attention irresistibly flags; for not only is such practice no good, but it encourages slack performance. This inability to attend, which besets almost everyone for a long or short period during a course of training, and is the arch-enemy to progress, is often the result of fatigue, genuine tiredness of muscles or nerves; the eye times a stroke incorrectly, or the overworked muscles are slow to respond. Now this condition should have been avoided; and most people who have suffered from it are perfectly aware that yesterday, or two days ago, they went on with their practice when something, eye, muscle, or nerve, distinctly told them: "We have had enough." However, here the condition is now, and there is only one remedy—rest. It is a bore, but it is your own fault.

This genuine tiredness must not be confounded with a symptom which certainly it closely resembles in its effects, but which appears to us to be really different, and may be treated with success by an opposite method: the symptom known as staleness. One is not conscious in any way of fatigue, the practice may easily have not been at all excessive, yet for the time all briskness is lost. Now though rest is recommended by many as a remedy for staleness, the opposite treatment—namely, continuance, if not increase of work—is worth a trial; and if one steadily and perseveringly plays through an attack of staleness, one usually emerges from it better than when one went in. It is a point on which trainers disagree, some recommending, as we have said, an emollient treatment—namely, rest; others a tonic. But above all, if you decide, rightly as we think, to play through your staleness, play with all the concentration and briskness you are capable of, and do not lay the foundations of a habit of slackness. Your best efforts, it is true, will produce deplorable results; but if you can harden your resolution to care nothing about the results, and hammer steadfastly along, an object of pity to men and angels, you will probably be the better for it. But if your resolution breaks down, and you relax from the poor best still possible to you, stop at once, for always and always slack practice is worse than none.

Another demon that, like the Promethean vulture, tears at the vitals of the man practising for a special event, or for general improvement, is the apparent slowness of the improvement, and at times its apparent complete cessation. Such a man, for instance, with the best intentions in the world will take out a handful of golf-balls to practise, let us say, mashie shots on to a green. The mashie is a weakness in his game, and the resultant positions of the first dozen shots cannot be covered with the traditional table-cloth. The next dozen perhaps are even less satisfactory, and at this point he will be wise to ask a candid friend if he is doing anything wrong; or, if the candid friend is a good player, to show him half a dozen shots. But it is quite possible that there is no obvious fault at all—only a general weakness. Then, having eliminated that most dangerous possibility—namely, of *practising a fault*, let this assiduous gentleman go on with his practice as long as he is brisk and attentive, and let him continue it every day for a week. Then, and this is the work of the demon alluded to, he may honestly think that he has not improved at all, and be disposed to label the principle of practice to a hot destination. But we solemnly assure him, if he has the least aptitude for the game, he quite certainly either has improved, though he is not conscious of it, or he has at least by his practice made some necessary steps towards improvement, and this improvement, when it comes, will probably be more rapid than he has thought possible. From being a poor performer with the mashie he will one day suddenly find that the club *has arrived*; that it has shouldered its way through the other mediocre performers in his bag and now stands predominant. But two postulates are required: (1) that he must be capable of improvement, (2) that he practises correctly.

Now this sounds a cheerful gospel, and will perhaps not be readily believed, especially by the person who is in the habit of telling one after a foozled mashie-shot that he always foozles with a mashie, and by way of showing how persevering he is, does not use the club again throughout the round, but plays improperly with an iron. And here it might be remarked, that though a match at golf certainly does give one practice it is by no means an ideal form of practice, any more than a set of tennis is an ideal form of practice. Indeed, it is even less ideal; for at tennis there is the fact that you are playing against an attacking opponent, to observe whom is no small part of the game, whereas one's real enemy at golf is not one's opponent, but one's own mistakes. Consequently, with the idea of winning the match one studiously avoids such strokes as may land one in such a position as to require the use of a shot which one knows to be weak, whereas in practice one should, instead of avoiding such a shot, do it a dozen times and yet another dozen. That is practice, and it is by such practice alone that the demon of despair is exorcised.

Another rule which applies to practice of all games is that the practiser should gradually increase the severity of his work, in proportion as the stroke becomes easier to him, till, long before his match comes off, he has become accustomed (in games of attack and defence) to meet a much fiercer attack than he is likely to be subjected to, and himself to attack with a ferocity which he will probably not need. This gives him the comfortable feeling during the match itself that he is playing within his limits. So, also, in golf-practice, let him by degrees increase the difficulties he must contend against, and no longer place the ball he wishes to play on to the green in as good a lie as possible, but in a rather bad one; and if his *bête noir* is a hanging ball, let him place for himself—after his initial difficulties are conquered—a dozen balls that hang not badly, but atrociously badly. Such practice as this will diminish his dread of such a hanging ball as he is probably liable to encounter, just because he has been in the habit of playing infinitely more poisonous ones.

Again, it is impossible to emphasize too much the value of the habit of sparing oneself as far as possible. You may be pretty certain that when the event comes off you will need all the nervous and muscular force at your disposal, and it is well to remember that the amount you have is but limited, and that although you have to play as effectively as possible throughout, there are many strokes which can be done with comparatively little effort in one way, but which if done in another are exceedingly tiring. For instance, the correct timing of a ball at tennis, and the bringing forward the weight of the body, using the large muscle areas to back up the arm, will drive a force or a boast with greater velocity than could have been attained by the arm alone, while the contribution towards fatigue and exhaustion thus entailed is infinitely less than if the forearm and wrist were taxed to their utmost.

It is the business of every trainer, and so of every one, for each man is his own trainer to a far greater degree than anyone else can be, to develop his individuality, and though certain broad rules can be laid down about the wrong way to do a thing, and in a less degree the right way, much should be left to natural aptness and facility. For instance, if a man can easily execute a stroke in a certain way with good results, it is impossible to say that such is not the right way for him to do it; for the orthodox "right way" may be very difficult to such a man, and it is mere waste of time for him to acquire it, if by another method he can accomplish the same thing easily. Here everyone can find out a great deal for himself, and since facility in movement is half the secret of success, he should, if he finds a real difficulty in executing some stroke in the prescribed way, carefully look about to see if he has not at his command some other method. It is idle, for instance, for a short, thick-set man to emulate a long loose swing at golf; he might as well practise high jump in order to be able to deliver a service at lawn-tennis from the height at which a taller man can, or practise the "split," in order to increase his reach. On the other hand, he has assuredly some advantage in his shortness that the long-legged man has not; it is this he must grasp and develop.

Finally, it is probably good for everybody to rest, if not completely, at any rate very largely, for a day or two before the event; for if a man is not fit then, it is highly improbable that a day or two more of severe training and practice will make him fit. On the other hand, rest—provided he does not fret—will largely increase his fund of nervous force, and his muscles already in condition will lose not one atom of their briskness by so short a repose. Again, the danger of over-training is far greater than that of under-training, and the risk of staleness or tiredness on the day of your match is far more likely, and, if it occurs, far more prejudicial to your chances, than the risk of not being quite at concert pitch. But if a man frets, he loses half the benefit that the rest would give him, and if he finds he inevitably does so, it is probably better that he should soothe his jangled nerves by employment. Yet there is a great, if commonly neglected, preventive against fretting, and that is the reasonable employment of the brain during the period of training. Then, when the rest before the event comes, it is easy to find distraction from the very natural nervousness, in mental pursuits, whereas if, as often happens, the period of training has been one of inaction for the brain, except in so far as the training itself was concerned, it is extremely difficult, if not impossible, to busy the mind with other and intellectual occupations. In fact, if only for the sake of the tranquil, not fretful, rest of the day or two before the event, it is well worth while, throughout the period of training, to have some definite and interesting piece of mental work every day. It should not, of course, be very exciting or very fatiguing, nor should the hours of work be so long that together with the physical preparation they produce fatigue; but nothing is a greater mistake than to drop brain-work altogether, not only, as we have said, for the sake of the rest before the event, which is practicably impossible unless the mind is otherwise occupied, but for the sake of the general flatness and utter want of interest in things after the day is passed. For the mind gets flabby and in ill condition if not used, just as the body does, while its reasonable use even during the most severe physical training cannot, we believe, have any ill effect at all on the body, for it is not in the nature of things that it should have; while if it has been unused for weeks, it is practically impossible to rest, as is strongly recommended, for a few days before the event, without fretting.

There is a sentence in the Latin grammar: "Too much confidence is wont to be a calamity." This is no doubt true, but it must be remembered that too little confidence is certain to be one; and though to inculcate a frame of mind is perhaps a useless task, yet there is, as it were, a correct attitude for winning, just as a straight bat is the correct attitude for a yorker, and it seems in the main to be this.

Never despise your adversary, but whoever he is treat him with respect. Cultivate a belief in your chances of winning, but remember that though you are not beaten till the last set has been finished, or the eighteenth hole putted into, yet neither is he. Husband your resources, unless things are positively desperate.

And so good luck to you. But if you have bad luck, remember you are a gentleman, or, if you are not, that you have an excellent opportunity for making other people think so.

CHAPTER X.

REMEDIAL.

WE have already spoken of the constant need of light, in order that the body may be healthy, and have suggested some simple rules about the use of heat, either in Turkish or ordinary baths. But these natural aids to health may, as we have said, be used as directly remedial agents in case of disease, or to correct existing bodily defects. Much scientific investigation has lately been made into the healing properties of electric light, whether used merely as light, or, as some hold, to put external electricity into the body; and it has been found to cure, not only weakness of the system, acting as a tonic, but even such tubercular diseases as lupus. We should not, however, recommend anyone to dabble with electricity, still less to go through a course of treatment except under skilled medical supervision, and this treatment by electricity comes outside the scope of this book.

Massage and rubbing, however, which can often be performed by a man on himself, are, for certain complaints, among those simple and excellent remedies which can safely be practised by anyone.[17] In the case of a strained muscle, for instance, in muscular rheumatism or lumbago, or when owing to some accident a man accustomed to exercise cannot get it, massage and rubbing are invaluable. In the latter case, the massage ought to be over the whole body, and so must be performed by someone else; but half the small local injuries which cannot well be avoided, can be greatly alleviated by such means, while an attack of lumbago or muscular rheumatism, which without such treatment might incapacitate a man for a week, can often be entirely got rid of by the employment of this remedy. The skin should be made soft and pliable by hot water, and any decent oil or embrocation may be used; not so much, perhaps, because it is in itself beneficial, but because the rubbing, which is beneficial, thus becomes easier to the manipulator, and spares the skin of the patient; for it is impossible to stand more than a minute or two of dry rubbing, if the rubbing is vigorous, owing to the soreness which it produces. In the same way, though the cause of lumbago (usually, if not always, connected with the liver) cannot be removed by massage, yet massage enormously alleviates the discomfort which often amounts to really severe physical pain. And half an hour's massage in the small of the back, a dose of uric acid solvent with every meal, and an abstention for a day from meat and alcohol may be sufficient to discharge most cases at any rate half-cured.

Another remedy we suggest—it is likely to be highly unpopular—as a cure for a very large number of disorganisations of the digestion or liver, is complete abstention from food, even for one meal only. For it is quite possible to be really bilious and yet feel reasonably hungry; but it is in such a case false to argue that hunger indicates food. In the same way a slight upset of the liver often induces great drowsiness, whereas to lie in bed sleeping inordinate hours is quite the worst thing to do. Nor is there any possibility of mistaking bilious-hunger or liverish-drowsiness for the healthy forms. It is even unnecessary to go into the point at all, for everyone knows quite well the difference between them. So if you are biliously-hungry, fast; if you are liverishly-sleepy, take exercise. It is possible, of course, that you need medicine, but try simpler remedies first.

Nervousness, that extraordinarily elusive foe to happiness, may arise from two causes, either from an overstrung condition accompanied by excitability, or from exactly the opposite cause—namely, weakness, and the need for tonic. In the first case—the two, again, are unmistakably different—it may be useful to try a less stimulating and irritating diet, and accompany it with plenty of exercise, followed by rest and muscular relaxation. In the second case, the same alteration of diet, substituting nourishing foods for the stimulating ones, and plenty of rest, with perhaps less exercise will be useful. In both cases, of course, medicine may be needful, but it seems to be almost a postulate in the question of health, to prefer, if that is sufficient, a perfectly wholesome *régime* without medicine, to the continuance of one that perhaps does not entirely suit you, with the addition of medicine. Medicine, no doubt, often is useful, and many of the nerve-tonics which so plentifully bedeck the pages of magazines that one would think that the Empire had an attack of nervous prostration, *may* be excellent medicines. But why take medicine, if as good results can be obtained without it? It is possible that you must—or at any rate think that you should—do more work than you can properly stand. If the duty is clear, and if it is also perfectly clear that you had better cheerfully give up the chance of working as well as you would like to work, unless you take a tonic, then by all means take a tonic which you know medicinally to be a sound medicine; but first see if there is not some possible means, such as alteration of diet, or, very likely, less stimulant, or a little regular exercise, of managing without that medicine. Strychnine, for instance, cannot be called an ideal food even in the smallest quantities.

Two other very common symptoms of some slight nervous derangement are restlessness and staleness. By restlessness we mean the disinclination often amounting to inability to settle down to any one thing. It is a particularly common symptom of the present day, when many people seem to be literally unable to have any fixed object of life, or to remain in the same place for more than a few days together. In acute forms this becomes a nervous disease of such seriousness that a regular rest-cure has been often prescribed—and with great success—for it: the patient goes to bed and stops there for several weeks, and is allowed neither to read, nor to talk, nor to make the smallest exertion that is avoidable. And in a less degree for ordinary restlessness the same treatment is applicable, and an increased allowance of sleep is desirable; or, if not of sleep, of deliberate rest; for the evil is due to over-excitation of the nerves without sufficient nourishment. And the nourishment of the nerves is repose.

Staleness, again, which we may define as a failure of co-operation between muscles and will, and which is most noticeable in athletic pursuits (since in ordinary life slight sluggishness in co-operation is not practically noticeable) arises also from fatigue of the nerves, due to excessive work, want of nourishment, or monotony of employment. To take the smallest imaginable instance, supposing two men, well trained in matters of eye, attempt merely to hit a lawn-tennis ball backwards and forwards over the net, as easily and gently as possible, they cannot keep it up for a quarter of an hour. Each stroke is simplicity itself, less than the A B C of the game. Yet by the monotony and tiresome iteration of it, their nerves get bored; there is no failure of muscular power, but they are *unable* to hit with the minimum of correctness after a very few minutes. Here is temporary staleness in its most elementary form, but it is some similar nerve-failure which is at the root of most staleness; incapability of correct work occurs without such fatigue of the muscle as would account for it; and to repeat the metaphor likening the muscle to the receiving instrument in a telegraph system, and the nerve to the wire through which the message passes, it may be a failure or a fault in the wire, though the instrument be intact, and the message (from the brain) be perfectly sent. That particular wire, or set of wires, must, therefore, be given rest, for it is mainly by rest that health and power come to nerves. In other words, change of exercise is required; or, if the whole system is a little out of gear, complete though temporary rest; or, again, a nerve-tonic may be needed; light, air, and cold water may set things right. Or, since the harmonious working together of all the parts of the body is conducive to correct work by any one nerve, it may be that the digestion is primarily at fault.

It is in connection with staleness that we may consider that daily and deadly enemy of strong and vigorous living—namely, Fatigue. If fatigue were nothing more than the natural and logical outcome of sound and healthy exercise of mind and body, the question would be simple enough, and we could take it offhand as one of nature's danger signals, enjoining rest. For it is one of the primary postulates that exertion must be succeeded by rest, and thus fatigue would be only the instinctive demand of the tired organs. But it will occur at once to most readers that the feeling of fatigue, anyhow, is in no way proportionate to the amount of exertion, bodily or mental, that has been undergone; more than this, bodily exercise, and in many cases mental exercise, instead of producing, actually seems to remove the feeling of fatigue. Clearly, then, the mere sensation of fatigue does not necessarily indicate the need of rest, or sleep, or food. A man, especially if he has dined late and heavily, may awake in the morning, even though he has had a good spell of sleep in an ill-ventilated room, feeling tired. Yet that feeling of tiredness is removed, not by further dozing, but by exercise, fresh air, or often brain work. But the contradiction is only apparent; there are, it is true, several forms of fatigue, but fatigue generally can be properly considered under one head. It will be necessary, however, to go back to a few simple physiological principles in order to make this quite clear.

In several of the simplest phenomena incident to life, we are utterly ignorant of processes. We know, for instance, for certain that we breathe in air rich in oxygen, and breathe out air full of carbonic acid gas. We know, again, that the proteid which we eat and digest and assimilate in our food becomes body-cells. We know that when we use our muscles we use up these body-cells, break them down and turn them into waste products; that when we use our brains some similar exertion of nerve is implicated. How these changes take place we do not know; that they do take place is absolutely certain, and it is in connection with these changes that fatigue occurs. A deficiency in the supply of oxygen given to the lungs is parallel to a deficiency in the supply of proteid given to the digestion; in both the organs are starved. Thus, to take the instance already given, the gentleman who feels fatigued in the morning, had better go out of doors; the longer he lies in his stuffy bedroom the more tired he will become. This is *one* of the causes of the fatigue from which he is suffering—namely, a starvation of his body in point of oxygen. He would feel fatigued in the same way, if he was starved in point of proteid. His fatigue, though he has taken no bodily or mental exercise for hours, and has been resting, is genuine fatigue consequent on an insufficient supply of oxygen. Therefore, he had better get out of doors, and take exercise so as to make up the deficit.

This unhappy gentleman whose case we are considering may have other causes of fatigue as well, even though he never takes any exercise bodily or mental, and habitually consumes large quantities of solid food. In fact, it is the food itself, with which he hopes to refresh exhausted nature, which is very likely tiring to him. He may habitually overtax his digestive organs, and almost certainly he will have in his system, owing to his sedentary and gluttonous life, a great quantity of waste products (among which is uric acid, the father and mother of gout), which in themselves are causes of fatigue. The system is clogged—the engine, so to speak, is running laboriously,[18] with all sorts of grit and refuse hindering the smooth working of its wheels and bearings. And this fatigue may be called chronic fatigue; as long as the excess of waste products remain in the system there will be disinclination for exertion, and fatigue rapidly ensuing on it.[19] The cure is to get rid of the waste products, as far as may be, by means of exercise, and by encouraging the system to throw them off by the action of the skin, the kidneys, and the bowels, and to remove the causes of the waste products in the future by avoiding those foods which are fruitful in them.

Now here, again, we find that what we may call healthy fatigue is surprisingly allied to this gluttonous fatigue, though in most cases, probably, the cure for one is the opposite to the cure for the other. The sedentary large-eater we should recommend, broadly speaking, to take exercise (extreme cases are liable to apoplexy, however), with a view to getting rid of his waste products. But it is the presence of waste products, also, which partly, at any rate, cause the feeling of fatigue in the man who has played a hard set at tennis, for exercise, as we have said, breaks down the body-cells which become waste products.[20] New cells, it is true, are, in the case of all healthy people tired with exercise, even then in process of formation, but the local fatigue of the muscles is largely due to the presence of these waste products, which the exercise has produced. Thus, strangely enough, the ignoble alderman is suffering from a cause closely allied to that which makes the open champion of the world at any game tired after his brilliant and successful defence of his title.

It is impossible in the small limits of a section to enter more fully into the physiology of this fascinating phenomenon, and we must refer the reader who wishes to know more about it to Dr. Alexander Haig's work on the subject,[21] and merely note that in this way exhaustion and so fatigue are brought about both by a want of food—temporary starvation—and also by an excess of food which causes excess of waste products. In the same way, too, though food may be needed, yet to bolt a heavy meal will not meet the case satisfactorily, since much of the nourishing value of the foods will be lost, as they will not be given to the stomach in a form in which it is possible for it to assimilate them, and also the digestive and excretive organs will be severely taxed, and fatigue in them will be produced.

As we have said before, fatigue, even when produced healthily, so to speak—namely by the exercise of muscles in the open air—may be quite disproportionate to the work accomplished. This question is dealt with under the chapter on exercise, and it will be sufficient here merely to mention that the wrong use of muscles (*e.g.*, slow heavy movements for the wrists as in many dumb-bell exercises), or the use of the wrong muscles, as, for instance, excessive employment of the muscles of the arm when what is needed is the use of the large body muscles, are common causes of unnecessary fatigue in games and athletics. There are, furthermore, many mental causes of general bodily fatigue, for in the intimate interweaving of mind and body, as we have seen, the one suffers with the other. Thus worry of the mind, nervousness, depression, make one feel physically tired, not because the muscles have been used, but because the nervous energy whereby they work has been exhausted by mental trouble. Here, if a man can bring himself, by an effort of will, to take an interest in some bodily or mental pursuit that will draw his mind off himself and his worry, he will quite certainly be the better for it, for the nerves that have been wearing and exhausting themselves over the trouble will have rest. And rest, as we have said before, is to nerves what food is to the stomach and oxygen to the lungs.

A common result of faulty digestion is a tendency to grow fat. Just as extreme thinness results from failure to digest food properly and so get the nourishment out of it, so a certain kind of obesity is likewise a wrong digestion of food; and though the symptom of "laying on flesh" is often ignorantly considered a sign of health, it may be distinctly a sign of bad digestion, if the flesh that is laid on is fatty. Certain foods, such as sugar and oil, are in themselves fattening; so, also, is starchy food, even if not properly masticated. An avoidance of excess of liquid is a good precaution against obesity, if under that word we class abnormal weight; so also is the habit of making the skin act properly by baths and exercises; so, too, are exercises for the abdomen, which facilitate the processes of digestion (though these exercises should not be employed when the digestion is at work—*i.e.*, just after meals). And everyone should remember that it is far easier to avoid getting fat, than to stop the process of accumulation of fat when once it has set in. Prevention here is not only better, but easier than cure. By a strange perversity of nature, fat people have often a craving for fattening foods. But this must obviously not be taken as a healthy instinct; it is an instinct of a diseased condition.

Another common enemy of health is constipation, and it is an enemy mainly because waste material, which should be ejected, is retained in the body, and during its retention necessarily disperses a certain amount of poisonous gases and substances through the body. But it is a question whether the drugs which many people are accustomed to take almost daily with a view to its prevention or cure are not as bad in their effects. And the sad thing is that an enormous amount of such constipation could be cured by perfectly simple and natural means. Diet is largely responsible for it; so, too, is the lack of exercises which facilitate the movements of the bowels. People who suffer from it should be sparing in their use of stimulants, especially of those which have a large percentage of alcohol, and in their use of white flour, and of flesh foods, the place of which should be taken by other foods, such as brown bread, tomatoes and fruit, fresh if possible, or stewed. These are without doubt the best preventives, and also the best remedies. Above all things it is most injurious to get in the habit of relieving constipation by doses of salts, or of other medicines even less innocent. The sort of diet which both prevents and alleviates it is a natural remedy, as also are the bending and leg-raising exercises which help the action of the bowels. They are worth trying.

But perhaps of all enemies to health, laziness is the most powerful and the most insidious. The health of any function depends, as Aristotle said long ago, on its energy; and to be employed is a better drug against most ills that flesh is heir to, than any that can be found in a chemist's shop. Whether it is headache you suffer from, or depression, or (if your malady is very acute) atheism or gout, the probability is that work, either bodily or mental, would have prevented it, and that work, bodily or mental, will cure it. For owing to this reaction of body or mind on each other, there is no doubt that boredom and discontent will actually produce indigestion, just as indigestion in the stomach will actually produce depression of mind. Again, to take a tiny instance, there are few people who would care to eat their way through a long dinner alone, but give them cheerful companionship, they will digest with avidity that which if they ate by themselves they could barely swallow. So also in bigger matters: occupy your mind always with any subject that interests it, provided it is not harmful, and as far as your well-being is concerned it does not matter what this subject is. If you ever feel bored, you may be quite certain that your boredom is in ninety-nine cases out of a hundred due, not to the stupidity of others, but to the stupidity of yourself. Stupidity of that order is one of the least admirable things in the world; and for the sake of your self respect try to be a little less of an idiot. However poor you are, it is probable that most things worth having, even Greek gems and fine music, are accessible to you, the one at the British Museum, the other at the Queen's Hall. Surely there is something in the world which involuntarily finds its way into your thoughts at vacant moments? Encourage that; work at it; get to know some thing worth knowing about it. Take a pride in your body if you will, you might do worse; get to play something passably; weight-lift even, if you really enjoy it, or if it leads you to a pride in your physique; do anything to be occupied. For this is the great remedy of all—work. It is certainly not worth while to sit and consider how noble you are and what few opportunities you have, nor is it worth while to sit and consider—except very occasionally—how base you are and how many opportunities you have. Instead, go and take one of them. *Do* something, whether you suffer from headache or atheism, *do* something, make boots—even very badly like

Tolstoi—or make history like Napoleon, or make geography like Livingstone. Whatever your age is, there should be something you like, which is not harmful. Do it, with both hands, for there is health—work!

THE END.

FOOTNOTES:

[1] Perspiration, it may also be noticed, regulates the temperature of the skin by evaporation. Thus on a hot day after we have cooled down from exercise we feel considerably less warm than before the exercise. "Text-book of Physiology," Schäfer, Part I., p. 669.

[2] These exercises, it may be added, bear no claim to be considered wholly original; many of them, in fact, are taken direct from other systems, especially the Macdonald Smith system, which can be heartily recommended; some few we believe are new. They are offered not as final or complete exercises, but as a selection from the best which we can give at present. Suggested improvements will be welcomed.

[3] "As certain as it is that a country walk through fine scenery is more invigorating than an equal number of steps up and down a hall, so certain is it that the muscular activity of a game, accompanied by the ordinary exhilaration, invigorates more than the same amount of muscular activity in the shape of gymnastics."—Herbert Spencer, in *Facts and Comments*.

[4] "Many men are attempting to carry the diet of youth on into middle life and age, or the diet that was quite correct for an active outdoor life into a life of sedentary office work in a town; or if they fall into neither of these errors they are generally completely ignorant with regard to the relative value and importance of foods, so that they either starve themselves on vegetables or herbs containing little or no albumen, or, on the other hand, overfeed themselves...."—Dr. Alexander Haig.

[5] For the question of milk-proteid in general, see *Text-book of Physiology* (Schäfer), Vol. I., page 135. For Plasmon, Hovis, and other simple foods, see *Muscle, Brain and Diet* (Sonnenschein & Co.).

[6] Though this really belongs to the Pulse family.

[7] On the part played by saliva in digestion generally see *Text-book of Physiology* (Schäfer), Vol. I., page 342, &c.

[8] On the excitation of the gastric juices by suggestion only, see Schäfer, *Text-book of Physiology*, Vol. I., page 349.

[9] "The process of training that has to be undergone by athletes nowadays is reduced to hard-and-fast rules. That these rules are not so good or scientific as could be wished is a matter for regret. The work of training is left to 'trainers,' and they are men who, learning from their predecessors whatever facts were known to them, build up a code of rules framed largely on imperfect experience, and added on to by what they themselves have believed to be useful. Medical men of reliable knowledge and sound professional attainments have seldom lent themselves to consider seriously the subject of training, and so place the subject on a sure scientific footing.... Many a man breaks down in training from being made the subject of some imperfect or unsuitable *régime*."—Dr. James Cantlie, in "The Book of Health."

[10] "To-day we take baths as a matter of course. Apart from the pleasure of washing and of having washed, we know that soft warm water can remove 'the dried-up epidermis or scarf-skin, the deposit of sweaty and oily matter, to say nothing of the dirt and impurities derived from the air and the particles rubbed off from our clothing.' But 'we realise with difficulty that the bath was but rarely met with in houses built even forty years ago. Bathing in those days, and therefore, of course, swimming, formed no portion of the school curriculum, the gradual introduction of first one, and then the other, being among the salutary results of recent educational development.'"—Dr. Malcolm Morris, in "The Book of Health."

[11] An open-air treatment can now be had at "Broadlands," Medstead (Hampshire).

[12] "Many think with Herbert Spencer [who, however, holds that 'imperfections of nature may be diminished by wise management'] that education is useless or almost powerless; that human evolution is ruled by heredity.... This modern conception, which accords to heredity a power at least equal to that ascribed by ancient poets to Fate, is assuredly excessive.... Education may

supervene efficaciously; it succeeds in giving birth to *artificial instincts* capable of balancing the hereditary instincts, and even of suppressing them; in short, of substituting for innate ancestral habit an acquired individual habit."—Professors Proust and Ballet.

[13] "In the earliest times of the human race ... to prompt people to take exercise meant only to induce them to do their daily work. In later times, however, and especially in the world of to-day as we know it, the multiplication of industries has placed many classes in such a position that exercise is something independent of, and has to be added on to, their daily employment.... The clerk at his desk and the merchant at his counter; the tailor in his crooked position and the milliner at her seam; the printer setting up type from morning till night; the workers, or rather watchers, at manufactories ... have one and all forgotten that their lower extremities are meant to carry them about.... Every departure (from the physically active life) may be an intellectual advance, but a muscular retrocession— a social gain, but a physical decline. Such being the case, it is evident that a great change either in the physique, or in the means of obtaining exercise so as to maintain that physique, must have taken place; and when we come to look at it we shall find that *but few of the employments of the present day carry with them a sufficiency of exercise.*"—Dr. James Cantlie, in "The Book of Health."

[14] In America the Y.M.C.A. Clubs are, we believe, almost invariably athletic, if not primarily, at least essentially.

[15] "There is method in walking, method in running, method in raising a burthen with as little effort as possible. The [correct] practice of an exercise leads then to a diminution of muscular expenditure, to an economy of work, whence results an apparent increase of the strength of man who does the work."—Dr. Fernand Lagrange, in "The Physiology of Exercise."

[16] "After a certain period of study difficult exercises have been learned, and may then become automatic. Their effects will then be very different. Is it not quite a different thing to *amuse* oneself with dancing from *occupying* oneself with learning dancing? Dancing, riding, rowing, even running, when they have long been practised, need no more [conscious] brain work than walking, which

is above all an automatic exercise.... It actually needs an effort of will to oppose an action which has become unconscious and to change an acquired pace.... We see at the first glance the great hygienic superiority [as increasing the oxygen in the system, removing waste products, relieving the brain fatigued by intellectual work, &c.] of exercises which can be performed automatically, with economy of nervous energy, complete [?] repose of the brain, absolute [?] inaction of the psychical faculties. The work of the human system is then performed by the coarser parts of the machine, and fatigue is first felt by the subordinate agents of movement.

"But for certain bodily exercises the period of apprenticeship is indefinitely prolonged, and the movements need an increasing guidance on the part of the nerve-centres and the conscious faculties, because these movements cannot be constantly identical, and unforeseen emergencies occur. Fencing can never become an automatic exercise, notwithstanding the tendency exhibited by certain parries and thrusts to become habitual actions and to be performed instinctively; the movement cannot always be performed in the same manner and follow always the same order, for they are subordinated to those of the opponent." Dr. Fernand Lagrange, in "The Physiology of Bodily Exercise."

[17] Of the value of exercise as a cure, the French nerve-specialists, Professors Proust and Ballet,[*] speak most emphatically. What they say about neurasthenics will apply in general to those who feel disinclined to move:—

"There is in truth no case in which muscular exercise should not figure under one shape or another.... There is a whole group of patients to whom it would seem at the first glance that all muscular work should be forbidden. Complete muscular inaction, however, would be as injurious to them as exaggerated work, and for them more than for all others the rule of progressive increase of work, of slow and methodical training, must be rigorously obeyed. They are perpetually on the verge of fatigue; their reserve of motor nerve-energy is, so to speak, *nil*, and the slightest *voluntary* movement is enough to exhaust them. Hence the only muscular work that can be prescribed to them, at first at least, is that effected by *passive* movements and *massage*, by which a whole series of muscular, tendinous, and cutaneous stimuli are transmitted by the sensory nerves to the cells of the centres ... these stimuli gently arouse the motor centres, and even the mental image of the movement aids in the same result, that is, in preserving the functional activity of the centres without tiring the patient. Besides, passive exercise and massage promote the peripheral circulation."

Dr. Weir Mitchell includes these, with faradic electricity, all three to be increased gradually, in his famous treatment for nervousness.

[*] "The Treatment of Neurasthenia." (Published by Henry Kimpton.)

[18] "The need for exercise is one of the numerous sensations which lead human beings to perform actions necessary for the preservation of life or health. The need for repose is called fatigue; the need for exercise has not received a special name, but deserves one quite as much as hunger, thirst, &c. Under the influence of deficient exercise, certain materials which should be used up each day by work, accumulate in the human machine, the wheels of which they encumber, and the working of which they clog.... It is necessary, for the perfect balances of nutrition, that the reserve materials should be used up as fast as they are formed." Dr. Fernand Lagrange, in "The Physiology of Bodily Exercise."

[19] "The fatigue which is due to dearth of albumens (proteid) in the blood is always absent so long as sufficient food is taken and digested; in the condition of dyspepsia mentioned in the previous chapter it was not digested.... If a man who has had a sufficient supply of albumens put in, and who has a good digestion, yet falls out in the early stage of a contest, long before those albumens can be exhausted, we must conclude that his fatigue is due to uric acid in the blood." Dr. Alexander Haig.

[20] "Similarly excessive exercise increases the amount of uric acid in the body."—*Text-book of Physiology* (Schäfer), Vol. I., page 595.

[21] *Uric Acid* (Dr. A. Haig).

Contents